W9-BQZ-915

CATRACHOS

CATRACHOS

Poems

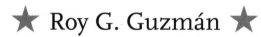 Roy G. Guzmán ★

Graywolf Press

Copyright © 2020 by Roy G. Guzmán

This publication is made possible, in part, by the voters of Minnesota through a Minnesota State Arts Board Operating Support grant, thanks to a legislative appropriation from the arts and cultural heritage fund. Significant support has also been provided by the National Endowment for the Arts, the McKnight Foundation, Target, the Lannan Foundation, the Amazon Literary Partnership, and other generous contributions from foundations, corporations, and individuals. To these organizations and individuals we offer our heartfelt thanks.

Published by Graywolf Press
250 Third Avenue North, Suite 600
Minneapolis, Minnesota 55401

All rights reserved.

www.graywolfpress.org

Published in the United States of America

ISBN 978-1-64445-023-9

2 4 6 8 9 7 5 3 1
First Graywolf Printing, 2020

Library of Congress Control Number: 2019949910

Cover design: Mary Austin Speaker

Cover art: Tamayo, Rufino (1899–1991) © VAGA at ARS, NY. *Hands on Blue Background* (*Manos sobre fondo azul*), 1979. Etching. 21¾ x 30 in. AC1997.LWN.1865. Los Angeles County Museum of Art, Los Angeles, California, USA. Photo Credit: Digital Image © 2019 Museum Associates / LACMA. Licensed by Art Resource, NY.

Para todas mis familias

CONTENTS

CATRACHOS

Time blunts the crooked / to savage pews / Once / on the sibling stumps / of a beat Caribbean pine / my cousins invite me to sit / My legs fold like melted candles / If I'd worn the maracas / -sizzled skirt of my reveries / their beamed liturgy: / *¡Maricón!* / *¡Maricón! ¡Maricón!* / Fold your hands / boy / walk straight / never graduate your hungers / Befuddlement sloths on their tongues / their eyes chapels of pebbles / We mount the izote tree / Tía Mamá watchtowers from the kitchen / a large pot of soup on the stove / pataste rapunzelled with dollars / Mom's MoneyGrammed early / in the morning / I heed to my accusers' orders: / Perch on the boulders our mothers / lay their clothes to mummify / jostle against the lengthy hammock / Abuelo bought en el mercado / They knot my wrists / with hands that have buried only mothers / I become their hummingbird embroidery / the ground on which their marbles rattle / like homemade rockets / Hopscotch squares sunrise on the sidewalk / Another underage infantry curls over / Nameless flowers ambush my scraped knees / I am the lasso / of a small emptiness / that once called me Almighty / I am pushed into the dirt hole / they dig for our G.I. Joes / rows of tanks / artillery / *He won't do it* / one cousin remarks / another one shouts / *You're wrong!* / Somebody wheedles me to sit / on a jagged set of stairs / For my performance / I smooth out the back pockets of my pants / my heady skirt / any creases might behoove punishment / When I hear a gasp / Another gasp / *Whose girl am I?* / I am losing my part-time voice / of a child / The rock-casters disperse / shoeless / like the sounds of shacks crumpling / under fathers / Flowers are plucked from the bushes / strewn on my knees / etiolated honeysuckles / The youngest pulls a chunk of grass / shakes his green-stained hands / unlatches blades from his fingers / I take a sniff of the carnations / I hear a chortle / This is my burial / à la Ana Mendieta / Through the window / Tía Mamá scrutinizes the hubbub / storms outside in her flour-caked apron / hands glistening / water drops penetrating their anticipation into the ground / She pulls me by the hair / in the house she unfastens my belt / strikes me with it / a newborn island on my cheek / the ghost of another body my body / For supper / she serves us bland / cauliflower soup / The scalding dam overfloods my throat / I avoid the white-meridian scalps / When I finish I ask for another ladleful / this appetite is now scratching the muted aqueducts / A folklore of vomit takes residence on my tongue / As my cousins turn to me / the spoons shine on their faces / In this fresh bodygarden / the tangerine trees release their grip / on the children from unforgiving floors / The little palms barely graze the ground / before they crash

QUEERODACTYL

We vogued in graveyards, headstones big
         as Daddy's factory plant, *Playboy* magazines littered
under the bathroom sink, sour cream drip-drops on our moustaches.
         No one knew whose mom had charred the tortillas.
We scraped marmoleum floors with our heels. Geometry
         went defunct, went apparel, berserk, bull in jeans, torero.
Our mothers neared their lips to our dirty claws
         as we swayed them in man's holy, unshaven catastrophes,
prayers so lit you'd think they went out to find a job. We
         no longer searched for food on the ground or in the sky.
Knew border by its shame. Plunged our bodies into it
         the way a father's hand might twist, tighten, rip a rosary.
Have we ever told you what else we felt when the earth's doors
         betrayed authority—when wind unfurled wig, crystal
beads, the sacrament in our hands? Had mercy shown up as mercy,
         we might have stopped the idealized throttle. Picked
our hips from the humid ground. Fashioned ourselves a new savior.

DÍA DE LOS MUERTOS

I.

On the eve   of mumbling saints   a gutted piñata   burns

in the pregnant   vision of an embrace.   I approach & dip

my drinking plastic straw   into the fire.   Someone else's birthday

sentence plays in the background—   cake at the edges

of our mouths.   Our parents sorrow gifts   like homeless magi.

Mosquitoes—   though we've christened them   *zancudos*

closer to *zánganos*   slackers   parasites   what our folks called us

—swivel with the charred   torn news of our despair.

II.

Boy with deer knees   like the mother I found dead one evening

on the side of a road under construction.   What are we

witnesses to   that implicates us   insufficiently?   Boy

with thick eyelashes   canonized in a white cotton dress   like

that side of honesty that misconstrues it   as cliché   but most

human   —the difference between failure & love   is where

you draw the incision—.   Boy in military clothing.   Boy in sinking

flotilla.   Through the straw   the fire burns my finger.

III.

Biblical row of mothers—   arms around their boys in the kitchen—

sleeves perfumed—   skin smooth as holy   water

before it stains.   In the boy's bedroom   our hairs parted

like maps looking for their rivers.   We carve out a canvas

from our fears   whispers—   intimacy of this kind is smoothed

with shovels by the police   now the military   —tell me why

I haven't stopped digging myself   out of this ground   —tell me

    when we'll pull our country   from that chalked potholed road.

       IV.

Every year we raised the dead   we thanked them for the floods

    thanked them for how the missing bodies   floated

when we planned to find them.   After a few beers   our fathers

    returned from their lovers' beds   bolted down our doors.

From an infantile zoo   we'd burst out running.   How many lives

    have I left ensnared—   lives still learning to stretch out

their shadows   —strategies to grow out   new mouths—

    consume only the heart of the deer   carry the rest home?

QUEERODACTYL

You don't have to watch me whip my wings
back & forth to count the number of fiyahs

I've put out. Single-handedly. Lady don't
PLAY. *Up-in-out—don't break your nails*

on that triceraTHOT! Out-in-up—
werk that bill! werk that bill! werk that bill!

Dudesteroid wanted to barge in here
all dudesteroidsplainy, all PCblazin',

but I was like, NOPE—.
You can't be going around preaching

that embers wash off more easily than glitter,
not if you're going to fry our camouflaged

nightgowns with your silicate dick complex,
exploding on every beach we go sunbathing on

like a bottle of Viagra roulette.
They used to call me Shorty for my short

appendages. But I ain't no chickenhead,
no duckhead. Don't confuse my bobbing,

my elongated lips, for submission, for a trick
daddy's mass extinction. *Lift that tail,*

swing that pitchfork, swing that tail, tail drop!
Momma Dearodactyl used to say that when

you deal with murderous jaws larger than yours,
you ought to multiply your fortunes

near an active volcano. Sniff the fumes,
swallow your enemy's offspring in one gulp,

go for the longnecks first—bigotry will claim
innocence even while it burns our sanctuaries.

Raptorhole. Tyrannohole. YouAintFly-
LikeMehole. To hell with dudesteroids

doing Triassic 4 Pay—the voyeur will always
miss the freedom of a red sunset.

Box dip, hairpin, mating squawk, shwam!
Cunty cunty cunty cunty cunty cunty cunty . . .

Don't let them know where you hide the rest
of your fangs—sis! Or that you're into fossil-

friendly excavation sites that can fit an entire
rainbow. So what if I have pycnofibers

on my back? Call me cub, call me bear, I ain't
roaring like a DinoKatyPerry. Bring it! I said:

Bring it!!! Now sashay . . . Dude'roid still
hoverin' in the sky—closet queen, angel dust.

In this ball of fiyah hate can't enter our ozone.
& for as long as the earth remains a hungry bae

there will be no death drive. We won't perish.
Our scaly spirits can survive in fields of magma,

don't they know? Silly hoes. Hoes that can't
even get into this party. HOES. No one's ditching

this bitch without leaving an impression: phoenixes
on the dance floor—thrusting in the face of loss.

ATONEMENT IN THE KEY OF PADRE

In one corner, the emptiness
    they call Father. In every other:

                    spilled blood.

How do you feel standing next to me, son?

        I hold out a torch to the man
        who crawls from my caverns

every evening. *Everyone in my family holds their breath.*

Father watches me wear a dress
of April showers in the kitchen.

            Black orchids—*He takes*
           a sip from his cerveza,

avoiding my gaze, wrapping one arm
around my brittle waist, his legs spread open
                  like a giver—

black orchids sprout from my mouth
as Mother walks in with her version of the house keys:

        three mute voices hanging
        by the throat

of the tree of shame. The tree of a thousand remorses.

Father is hunger. *Nothing, I tell him.* Father
is obsidian knife. *Nothing.*

Mother can tell which visitor I am hiding in the bathtub.

        Broom in hand,
    she is ready to sweep the cinders

            back to the furnace.

I lie to him so I can live.

OUR LADY OF SUYAPA

I believed in our Lady of Suyapa before I believed in the Phoenix Force,
in her opaque gold aura of an 8, in the 12 mojados above her distended

coronet of erupting, devalued lempiras. Before I believed in possession,
I learned when to vanquish the barbarous eyes of those who crave

universal forms—platonic adversaries. Anchored against the loss
of flesh, a hand or a skeleton. I knew resurrection before I knew death,

identified the hazardous chemicals that equaled higher wages, my mother's
lungs gone AWOL, a hacking in the meat sky, arid the reverberation.

I have cast eclipses from my house of tremors, only to find them revived
under the floorboards upon my return—the tricks perception pulls

as when night consumes a nebulous man, a star's stern birth the kernel.
Nothing touched is ever sacred unless it's robbed first. Our pilgrimage

involved hewing the country our knees purported, scabs & breadcrumbs
befitting a pigeon's throat. No sacrosanct architecture without lament.

When Cyclops holds whatever angle of immortality can perish
in issue #136 of *Uncanny X-Men*, we run into grief that aspires

to exist as nothing more than grief. Smoldering shadow of the Phoenix
as quintessential disaffection, onslaught, either slaughter or sainthood,

stateliness or snapped wire. In every uniform seal the stranded
feather of an extinct bird. Which is what I meant to show my mother

when I led her down the staircase of vine handrails within my crypt—
though she shrieked that love like mine is nonviable, holding a plate

under the hot tap water, as if to stand on thin ice past the season's rotting.
For now, outlines. For now, letters of grief inside church domes

in lieu of tonsils. *You are no longer a virgin*, he rustled as I guzzled
his entire pool of handsomely green leaves, as if the Minotaur's myth

had been unwarranted. What conviction will foment in the exoplanets.
I trusted servitude before belief, the fires that cavalcade without pageant.

But those ashes: how they gather in the faceless ether—masterless gloom-
glowers remarking, I'm not from here. When & why would I leave?

MY GREAT-GRANDMOTHER'S EGG THIEF

was never officially charged   though she considered her son's
    wife prime suspect   Rita   my great-grandmother's
name   never trusted her daughter-in-law   & maybe
rightfully so   Mamachela's hazel eyes & light skin   as myth goes
    two reasons a man would let   his Trojan horse loose
    though in this case   after the third child died   she left
my grandfather Jorge   to raise four more   found another
home with a soldier   a newfound pariah status   which is why
    when I took a drama class at the University of Chicago
    & we were studying Ibsen's *A Doll's House*   the renowned
British actor who cotaught the course   was appalled when I said
    Nora still had a future to look forward to   even in the 19th
century   surely white feminism   never met the Latinas in my family

                                                            & few

things match the warmth of an egg   right after it's been laid
    During summer   eggshells babble   on the ground
    the evidence of a predator's mischief   a branch-buttressed
nest's disposal   or a bird content with gravity's assignment   A man
was jailed four times   for stealing 700 rare wild bird eggs:
    ospreys   golden eagles   red kites   peregrine falcons   merlins
    redwings   avocets   In his residence / maps   climbing
equipment   camouflage clothes   miniscule holes drilled
on the shells   *Thou shalt not steal*   *Thou shalt not covet*
    thy neighbor's wife   Not the contents   but the collectible casings
    How do you return   everything you've stolen
from us?

Control the thing   you most love   at the root of your addiction
    Folks camped outside Rita's house   to have their tarot cards
read   before she aged & forgot   who she was   forgot how to bathe
    reeked of piss   chicken manure   eau de cologne   To schedule
a consultation   men rolled from under cars   stars in their own
Cantinflas films   greasy hair   crème fraîche in the corners
of their mouths   the women gossiped incredulously   after flattening
corn on clay ovens for their patrones   matriarching all the ways
    we'd outlast the policies of the rich

The thefts of Rita's
favorite hen's brown eggs   the source of fantastical tales
    populated by ghostly   headless horsemen   who abducted
children if they ran   away from home   or women
    pregnant with black magicked frogs   or that man with a limp
deemed hideous   from false accruement   During sessions
    I'd climb the long vines   of Rita's backyard tree
    swing eight feet from the ground   with the visitors' children
    one of us would plunge   rip a new skirt   a striped shirt
passed down three generations   Our mothers would scare us
by paying my great-grandmother handsomely   for a remedy
    to exile our demons   once & for all   *Leave them alone*
she'd yell at them   *They're just kids!*

                         Years later I think about
Rita's backyard   the trees that once swiveled   their branches
near the ground   *It's none of your business what I do with my life*
    I hear Rita say—   daughter of an Indigenous woman
    & a man who   like most men in my family   left his breath
on everything   we call mirror   or past   a man who tried
to rape Mamachela   his daughter-in-law   some say he did
    Rita—   who bought land   with her own savings   a rare
feat for a woman in those days   in a country
where women can lose their heads if they dye   their hair
the color of a gang's affiliation   Rita—   who lost
    most of her land to the government   on which Tegucigalpa's
airport was built

                    which means that in the lines   of my wide
nose   my plump ears   my dense lips   I bear the burden
    of every arrival   every departure   my great-grandmother
    who resisted losing her memory   but lost it anyway
    as her son lost his   kicked in the bath   spat out the spoon
    concocted spells so potent   Indigenous secrets   mixed
with loss   which sojourn parallel   the strength of a thousand
stolen acres in her   the rest of us are still trying   to figure out
why she shakes our houses at night   when we all stood there
    in silence   watching her track the bandit's clues   not knowing
all of us were stealing her eggs   all of us hungering for love

QUEERODACTYL

Crude oil gushes out her lumbar piñata.
Tektites buck to a spiked
prerecorded message from bill collectors. Momma

Dearelict is our fossilized lark's fanciful enterprise.
Black whip of a dress bullying memory. Dermis
rubies hammered on tortilla forehead;

neck amulet tittered; lips framed by consecrated
hush. Whatever she gestates, a pioneer's
command. Whenever someone's child dies

it is unclear who dies. Even at the cusp
of obsolescence, she hummingbirds
against the lightning-loaded whistle of his slop

-py elimination—blackmailer soliciting
to spit his livestock anyhence, such
incompetent workmanship. Lotería dazzler,

star-forming dissolution. History is who buries
whom first. Mother all that burns
in holy water. What cradles. What deplumes.

PREPARATIONS FOR A TRIP HOME

1.

Almost a year before buying plane tickets you need to call everyone
who was good to you the year before, says Mom, setting blue plastic
Walmart bags next to brown boxes on the table. If anyone gave you
the evil eye or tried to steal your man, she says, or didn't offer you
a helping hand when your ass was unemployed, you cross them off
the list & with the names still left you pull out the old agenda &
call every number to see who's still alive. A few *The number you have*
reached has been disconnected notices later, Mom supposes you died
or they caught your ass & deported you. It's like going down a list
of those who play La Chica, or a raffle, but for paranormal reasons
"didn't want to claim their prize." *Quizá se los tragó la tierra*, my aunt
says, though the earth has no business with them. Or with us.

2.

La Chica is the everyman's name for the Honduran national lottery.
You buy your tickets at the pulpería or any other store at the mall
if you can afford a big bowl of seafood soup, un sopón. Every Sunday
we would gather around the radio & listen for the winning numbers,
turning down the volume of my grandfather's other radio that played
a marimba program, including interpretations of the Beatles' catalog.
Sometimes the price would go from one lempira to five lempiras,
depending on what was up for grabs. You could gamble for a toaster,
although mostly everyone still preferred tortillas. But there were times
when you could wager on a telephone & finally have a way to communicate
with your brothers en La Yuma without having to use your neighbor's phone
—the one neighbor who had lived outside the country & recently came
back all sick to live out the rest of her days in Honduras—if you won.
Nowadays, PlayStations are quite popular. Even a washer machine
is one way to slow down the blisters on your fingers from washing clothes
en la pila. But you won't find any rifa that goes for a lempira or twenty.
All you hear from everyone's mouth is *Dólares nos dan más pisto*. More dinero.

3.

¿A cuánto está el cambio? my mom typically introduces herself
at the currency exchange kiosk without even saying good morning.

I was in a rush, she tells me when I bring it up at home. Ay, no! my sister
can get a better deal in Honduras if I send the money directly through the bank.
With the way she counts money, dollar after dollar, I know the lady
at the kiosk is lynching my mom in her head. You've got to learn
where to get the best deals, hijo. No nos hagamos los brutos. We leave the premises
—a beep usually goes off to remind those of us who, like my mom,
are prone to carrying weapons inside the store to listen:
We're watching you. Nobody's bruto up in here. Puchica, ni que les
estuviéramos robando a estos sinvergüenzas, mom says, but I know that
if you find my mom with el moño vira'o, as my stepfather says, on
the wrong day, you may have a bounty hunter before you.

4.

Mom crosses out names like items already purchased at the supermarket
or comestibles too expensive for her temper. She still takes
my red pens from my bag when I'm not looking. Because I teach English,
my mother wants me to translate for her what the operator says when she
places a call, & for reasons of extreme alarm, she can't get through.
Come hear what she says. I write everything down & she runs her eyes over it
to make sure she understands a few words. What happened to Priscila?
I haven't heard from her in years, she says, briefly going to the kitchen
to check that the rice hasn't burned. I don't know how many times
I tell her I don't know. Why are plane tickets that expensive? I don't know,
the economy. Did Maritza go last year without taking something on our behalf
to my dad? I don't know, she doesn't strike me as someone who would
do that, Mom. She looks at me suspiciously, testing out how much of what
I say is based on speculative truth. Ya, dejá! Let me make the calls myself.

5.

We head to Walmart & there's a toy for a little girl whose mother
used to bring me toys when I was a little boy but, of course, I don't recall
the mother's name. Ten bags of rice are always discounted at Costco,
especially when you translate their cost to the exchange rate. Uno
mas uno por nueve. See how you can save a lot of money shopping here, hijo?
I'm usually in the aisle with the best-selling books when she approaches,
almost knocking me down with the shopping cart. Tomato sauce
cans are her favorite because we arguably make the best spaghetti
in Honduras, & she skips the tuna section because that's for the poor
& everybody's already tired of eating that over there. She finds garments

to wrap each item, including anything that isn't breakable. You can't trust
those zánganos, especially when you're at the airport & they're inspecting
every detail in your bag like you just stepped out of prison. Once the list is finalized,
the months roll by, one after the other, long months of anticipation,
of who's going to be nicer to her, who's been an exemplary grandchild
to my grandfather, who's going to be shocked that she's lost a few pounds.
Because I can't afford to skip work, I drive my parents to the airport.
My mom refuses to shed a tear, says, Nadie se ha muerto.
For a second, I think they're my children.

6.

She asks me how I'm doing over the phone. Why haven't I given her
a call? She didn't need one anyway, she reminds me, too busy catching
up with old friends, people she hasn't seen since they were in prep school.
I listen intently because she's about to give me a list. What do you want me
to take back home? Queso? Mantequilla? Beans? Torrejas (even though it isn't
Christmas)? That candy you used to eat as a kid, what do you call it? She doesn't
stay long on the phone, says she doesn't have enough minutes left
on the calling card, even though she just bought a magicJack before leaving,
but she hasn't been able to set it up. Skype doesn't exist either
because my cousin is always at work & doesn't have time to download it.
What did you eat today? she asks, all of a sudden concerned
she's missed the most important question. We'll see each other soon, I reassure her.
I know what I hear in the background is a celebration for no reason.
My absence is a faithful guest of honor.

MIDWESTERN SKULLS FOR THE BROKEN LATINO

People who crave the jaw
& not the fox's gentle tail—
     his land mine

     of teeth; a temporary exit
for those who yearn to return to the coyote's
       tent to reclaim their belongings—
the chopped head, the neck
before it was plucked from the rest of the body
like a hen's for dinner. Antique shops

     for raccoons' clawed feet;
             a necklace
for women in labor. After the snow melts
the dead return to their natural habitats—
eyes barely shut under the charcoal, whiskers
          trapped in the pinecones.
Some secrets are better rolled into the mouths

     of strangers
     while they sleep. A father can make up
suffering's seasons: leave in the afternoon,
then sneak in through a windowless frame—

though these, too, can be called winter & fall
     & held by a child's contemptuous hands
in a garden where only the wind
can be torn from branches.

          Did they really mean
to leave us shipwrecked—those sailors
who recognized flesh but not what the flesh
       can camouflage? People covet

the mandible as it's handed down
     for all to drink from. In his hands
I appear dead—
but here, here in my chest, is where my father
     finds the new continent

    of directions measured in forgiveness.
I sleep in the wilderness,
like a fox loitering in a frozen meadow,
                    & I'll feed him forgiveness
                        if he asks.

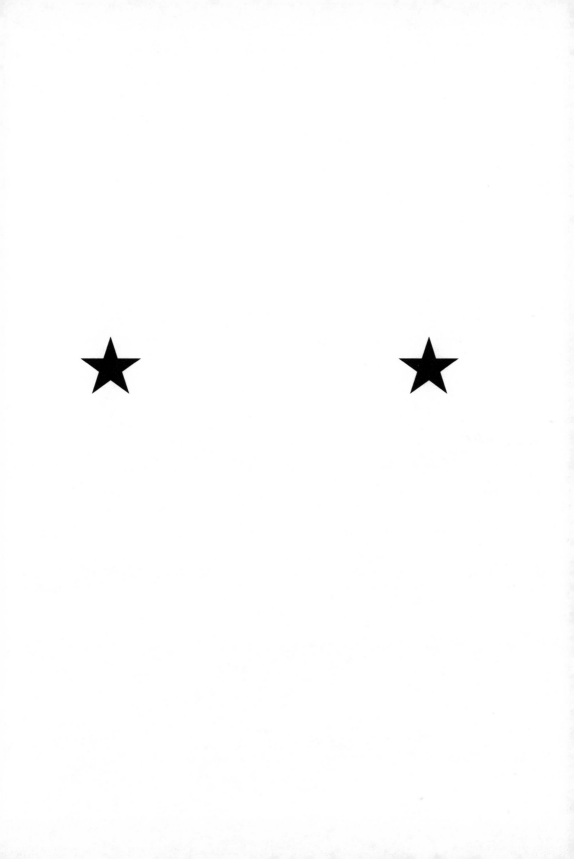

THE AMERICAN DREAM

I rest my head on my mother's lap
at the bus stop in Allapattah. Two rides
until we reach the first house, pass
the most untroubled labyrinth of palm trees
for the second, the third in the afternoon.
Roosters have yet to birthmark their morning
in another country. An alligator gasps.
As we disembark in Miami Springs,
our crises yawn like lonely sons. Half an hour
& the white children will awake. Mami whispers
her day's planned chores to me. Boleros stir
the kitchen's sanctity. Our patrones carry
their lunch packs to the car, fasten all
the seat belts. For a moment, we turn this into
our transitional home, spray the untrained
chemicals on every counter, their mirror
our mirror. I play with droplets on my arms,
a mixture of bleach, no gloves. Haven't we
already gambled our future kingdom—& lost?

On the stove the kettle squeals like schoolchildren
during recess. That is an image I'm willing
to defend. My mother's hands become two
mummified prayers that can't recall
their ancestral song, obsessed with leaving no dust
on the vintage couch, the oblong table, Barbie's
large house. If I take a hand before it can graze mine,
it blanks out on what it meant to verse me in,
too absorbed consuming the anxiety of surfaces
fixed on appearing young & debutant. I breathe
the Pine-Sol oil's direct ancestors. Someday, I say
to myself, I'll resent the nature of wood
for its suffocating fresh air, for its prolonged cruelty.

We work for families who don't own dishwashers,
but even if they did, my mother's pride
won't let her sacrifice her cleaning merits
by studying the electronic usurpation of what
her hands can very well do. It takes us long to finish

each house. A smile graces her face after
we upturn the others. For now, we're a team.
I rarely meet anyone older than five.
In muscular isolation I develop my own
fabrications with the plotlines of a precocious
loner who picks up books in English to learn
what to call each appliance, the angles of an expensive
bathroom, what snakes inside master bedrooms.

In my undrafted bill of child workers' rights
I am instructed to devote my livelihood mastering
with words what I can't apprehend with my silly
rough hands. By the end of each work day,
other mothers cough the same tragedy.
Single women sleeping in tiny bedrooms
where their landlords overcharge for dinner.
At the bus stop pants camouflage varicose veins.
Women flaunt a proud catalog of grandchildren.
If they trust you, they'll share what they get paid.

Some patrones are less cruel. But for every
fridge with full access, another has specific
precautions on the door. I am the only child
who goes to work with his mother—the others
haven't saved enough money to pay a coyote.
Sometimes we share Berguer Keen. Sometimes
Maldonal. Under a managerial sun, we revolutionize
the concrete benches with our tired asses,
exhume stories of lands we are too afraid
won't recognize us if we ever go back. Because if we do,
it'll be against our will. Because our grandmothers
require insulin. Because those grandchildren
need school supplies, an education. If we rise
tomorrow my mother will tickle my feet to hop
in the shower. A bowl of warm milk will greet me
at the table. On our way to the bus
we will worship our bodies in hush.

ALLAPATTAH BRANCH LIBRARY

I prance out the library with fifty English-slobbering gargoyles,
the limit, Catholic roars loudening from unconfession,

tablets of oxidized graters lugged under my arms.

Though I can't decipher the theme of green cards, I can
make legible the rough breaths of a brontosaurus, his fistfuls

of I did not choose this lifetime to be broken bys & the

marine ambivalence that smuggles legs for a profit—all those
dyes unclassified. Late fees & a lash. My parents

relinquish me reluctantly at the library. A block away,

a high school I avoid by pledging allegiance to my own
parenthood. A pawnshop, an AutoZone, a Western Union.

Churches pitchfork the sky like emblems of our cul-de-sac

utopias—& I, still unconvinced by the argument that salt
is the fitting mineral to symbolize misfortune, its chemistry

the place for what could not be gathered. O, cadaverous

Olympus: a resemblance of the Social Security office,
an abandoned warehouse, a taquería, a bodega that shut down

after the store was raided & its owners deported, a fill-in-the-

brown-inmate correctional center. My herbivorous giants
reproaching the carne asada whiff, a jury of dragonflies

slackening up the crisis of my tongue. Stegosaurus.

Brachiosaurus. McDonald's Happy Banquet. Department
of Children & Families. Figures of paginated hypotheticals

torrented on the futon, around my mother's egg-fossilized

bean soup. Ersatz adolescence. New measurements:
a skyline of silence, a footprint of unauthorized colloquies

in mismatched Spanish, a post-Pangaea of intimacies. I am

the paleontologist of a violence a library card attempts
to gyrate toward the imagination. How does one retire

one's taboos when the spotlight has hit one's face?

Sit still, my spawning seraphim. My insolvent chupacabras.
No matter how many more pages we authorize, they'll be used

for our burial. It's not a joke to ask for clemency to be taken

for alive. Query the neighborhoods that couldn't digest us,
or money's somnambulist banks. Stop sniffing that tome,

my clammy roaring rocks. For every lariat snatched

from my body's detonations, a father returns. If I let him stay,
he folds into the smell of an old book. When I say I've burned

my unabridged grammatology, I've breathed nothing

but dust from solitude's blues. Towers of absentees. Harem
of my predilected misnomers. Dios, what a cesspool of prospects!

QUEERODACTYL

Jewelry boom box spittin' *bidi bidi bom bom*
he verges his groove of slapstick smoke

across our donated mosquito nets *bidi bidi bom*
bom all night he fingertips our omnivorous junk

in his cruel maw of tooth gaps magical realistic
funky-ass choral arrangements of servitude mighty

dump truck hip-ee hip-ee dales my rotunda all
over these unsullied shimmies *bidi bidi bom bom*

orb-spider thighs cloaking his genocidal hunches
Momma catapulting protection abracadabras

over our twiggy panoplies we painstakingly
bedecked how many times haven't we fallen

for mishandled precipices in the wrongheaded
entirety of machomanic evacuation asteroid

in mouth-crooked chaps guayabera deep-pink
guava pulp rum & Coke in his fierce prayerful

grip to bypass civility a Google-translated wink
inumbrated eyebrows to cast embered mercies

I pump *bidi bidi bom bom* hormonal harmonies
for his jawlined mitzvahs *bidi bidi bidi bidi bidi*

on wings only light will kerfuffle flight born
at his bidding va-voomed for his favor we puff

from the tail of his pickup truck we clothes-
line an underwater continent marooned & whiplashed

for genesis if carnage can charade competency
we too can corrupt castanets timbre compulsory

penances over his padded knees *bidi bidi bom bom*
above his life insurance policy rates coma

with anointed vanity with the right song a stone
will pass for bread break for a fool's sunrise achieve

the love ritual cut scorn's willy bob hither to this bomb

ARTHUR'S SPELLING TRUBBLE

Jenna is asked to spell *essential*. She trips before Arthur is challenged with
aardvark. He freaks out: *What am I going to do—what am I going to do?*
Arthur rolls his arms, swings in his blue jeans & yellow cotton sweater,
sings out each mellifluous letter, as if memory held the body accountable
for demonstrating the ritual of remembrance. Gets it right. With only a year
of ESL, I win my school's spelling bee. I spell *platypus* correctly, though
I can't conceive of a platypus. I know *plate*; I know *pus*. My mother works
three jobs to pay for my tuition because the people we clean houses for
claim it's better than getting beat up in public school. I come home
with a bloody nose nearly every day. The school's denomination is Lutheran,
so we memorize Luther's Small Catechism, forever confessing sins
in hushed purgatory. It's private like the school I attended in Tegucigalpa—
you can't get a decent education otherwise—& my mother reminds me
where to mark accents on Spanish words, like crossing off memories I'm losing
from lack of access. *Just imagine a clock*, she says & the altar behind me vibrates
when I am assigned the word *platypus*, picturing it in my head as if I were cutting
around it with a crude pair of scissors. I am not expected to win; to everyone's
knowledge, I don't speak sufficient English. Arthur advances to the finals,
but he doesn't want to represent his class at the school-wide SPELLATHON.
Mr. Ratburn thinks I can do it, he shares with his family over a simple dinner.
If only all brown children had similar mentors. I begin gorging on new words.
Hood nomenclatures. I learn their roots but never my own. I spell *platypus*
& even the pastor's wife can't trust her ears. Afterward, the certificate bears
my name in sloppy ink over marker. Maybe she was starting to write down
someone else's surname when I was declared champion, or maybe she wanted
her son, who's in my grade, to make a comeback & win the title. He's blond
& I have a crush on him because I can see all the veins through his pale body;
he excels in every subject, that's what everyone expects of him; I receive
the same grades, but that's not expected of me; literature is the subject
that persistently keeps me off the honor roll. I keep looking up words from
Romeo & Juliet in the dictionary but my dictionary isn't smart enough.
Inadvertently, I'm looking up contractions, abridgments. Contraction: *C-O-N-T-
R-A-C-T-I-O-N. Contraction.* As in establishing a contract with anything that
dwindles; as in new disease; as in unplanned childbirth of words. *Platypus*:
from flat-footed. The schoolmate who called me *fag* behind my back enrolled
in the Marines around the time I signed up. We'd train as a unit. I'd look over my
shoulder, paranoid that, given the opportunity, he would out me. He was flat-footed,
was never deployed. Faggot: *F-A-G-G-O-T. Faggot.* The majority of us recruits
were the first to land in Iraq & Afghanistan, primarily poor, sons of refugees,

to die abroad as if dying on US soil wasn't already effortless. *They are not looking
for brown minds but brown war machines,* my stepfather says. The beauty
of machines is that they can be disassembled & reassembled. D.W. says, *I'm not
a prisoner of my vocabulary*—but I can spell anything that prays for my destruction.
A palindrome is a word that has two chances to disappoint you. There came a point
when I was so pedantic & territorial with words I couldn't finish full sentences.
Spelled words in my sleep. Embalmed my thoughts. I watch *Arthur* when I'm sick,
to my past lovers' chagrin. *Cartoons are too infantile,* they say, like parents who dab
hot sauce on their children's fingers to discourage them from thumb sucking.
They can't see which episodes I've hidden my luggage in, kept my dog-eared
thesaurus, my musty diplomas like diplomats to intercede for me when my accent
is called out, as if my tongue held lesions unconscious to me. *What dictionary
are you using?* the Brain says after he misspells *fear.* Fear as a part of speech.
Synonyms: transgressions that can only be found in mirrors. *Can you use it in
a sentence?* I was applying eyeshadow when my cousin stumbled into the bedroom
my mother & I slept in. I must've left an afterimage in the mirror, smeared with
a brown boy's thick eyelashes, a shade of blue to enrapture other brown boys,
as I turned around to stare into her eyes, ankles shaking in my mother's pumps,
hands behind me, as if handcuffed. I slipped the cosmetic through the narrow
gap of a drawer, half the heels trapped under the chiffonier. A broken TV
screen. In the episode, Arthur, in his round brown glasses, polytonal specter, sings
letters to a word that might define him. My parents aren't home yet. I rub
VapoRub on my temples. I'm back at the Lord's table, mispronouncing the wild
dream that finds me in a language that I might speak, from which I might drink.

QUEERODACTYL

Bones classified as those of a seafarer. Nimble
limbs that commanded pressure, searched
after water.
        For now we'll say this languid metaphor
of blood is inconclusive; that it is unimaginable
for the body to be opened twenty times in a row
without a parliament of owls
             hooting inexhaustibly
throughout the night. & what of the recognition
of one's voice as it's issued from an unused tunnel—
a martyr searching for salvation in no-man's-land?

How unfaithful
        the echo must be to its source, to the
metallic whisper in a cave of handprints, songs of
resistance, a vulture ingesting a carrion bird midflight.

A crime scene sketch artist renders the image
of an asteroid as it makes contact with the ocean
that is the body.
        From where the falling star buries
its head into the earthly bosom, a photogenic tsunami
erupts. Tragedy
        is where undefined county lines
congregate, where woods abut gravel roads. When
your body was dumped a pregnant doe leapt. Her eyes
beamed. Her hooves recited a pink aurora.

MARROW

They called you | Sarah | before you reared
the groundless Marrow | a craterous fill-in- |
the-blanks | orphan of the exterior | bone-

spangled banner | We are the incarnations of beauty
that burgeon | from exaggeration | the femur |
for the sunflower |the pangaean frontal bone

for the Rockies | Our countries | anywhere | jawless
apertures | ossified cathedrals | the bodies never
recovered | Their tonsils | how they distress us |

how the wolverine will drink | its image | & leave
behind | a childhood between | the land mines |
Our Father | *who art in arroyos* | *let us not*

be engulfed by our own | *bodies* | How did *struggle*
become de rigueur | for announcing the sharks'
premature oral fixations | Our flesh-fortresses

the new prairies | the husks of an unturned ocean
ulcerated from below | You are need | child
in captivity | the writing in the unpurified water

mere honey | spilled on saguaros | Your spears
the condemned bones | the crux | of the almighty
grief | If I break | my silence | the storm | colossal

QUEERODACTYL

Mother is anti-devolution, present past
unfuture, & we're at that stage where eating
spoiled flesh is like going to Las Vegas—
mercurial swimming pool of naked bodies.
Outside, cop is ash, cop is unopened bag
of glitter you take back to Walmart
for a refund. What do you call a corpse
the ocean's forgotten to bring back? So much
is layaway canticle, mended whisper, faux
pas de bourrée, braided feathers—it's no
wonder Spanglish is caged thunder, oblivious
certitude of orchids. Believe the coffee
grounds when they speak of banana
plantations. Before we left the house,
our mothers should've warned us of mirrors
paginated like bibles. The beat under the floor,
invertebrate possibility waiting to blast,
armoire with dresses befitting queens,
salacious cinderellas. When we were laid,
fist came before the egg. Today, no broom
is back-broken. Mother is howl-unshuttered
slats. That moment when the diggers
can hear the infant cry of desperation under
the city rubble. We run for the exit,
but we're really running for the interior
kingdom of fossils, how tenderly my mother
paired the socks & tied them by the neck.

AMOR ETERNO

The gray, chipped wall you stared at

murmured. You wore

      your bruises with honor.
                        Verbenas
        encircled your abdomen.

Kidnapped by four men
with masks as old as their faces,

                      you escaped.

They betrayed you.
Men repeatedly disappear
           behind the faith

       of a brother's cruelty—

     in the rancid smell
of torture. Eight days later,
             shot
       as you walked downtown.

In the morgue for hours

before police lifted the dust
       from under your shadow.

       Impunity.

At fourteen,

     you contracted the virus.
     The headlines said

the irony was that it didn't kill you,
         but that bullets

at night
        emerged like shooting stars in need
                of shelter.

                          Homeless

with a father abroad—
because all our fathers dream
                of misplacing us—

    you asked for asylum,

died
        before it was approved.

How many brown bodies will give up
                    their bodies

   so other brown bodies
       might live? In all the interviews

your mother said
you were not her biological son

             but felt

as if she had carried you
      in her belly

    just like her other two.

                  Where we were born,

corpses are left to bloat
      on examination tables. Roaches

          crawl
from the blossom
             of justice. *Our work*

here is done, they broadcast,
                              squirming like gods

               in despair.

If they've learned one thing about nurture

it's that a wound
                    often is the last thing

        urging for healing.

IN SERVICE OF SILENCE

[PROCESSION]

Children with church-pressed silence slapped
between their hymnals. Patriotic hush to build
character. A boy stoops to cradle donated
pumpkin soup, his spine marionetted through his silky,
lassoed hair—the grip of a locksmith versed in gospel.
Wax gag, stained-glass gag, raise-funds-for-the-steeple
gag, elementary gag. Swallowed sundown, the hearts
beat their tin-can drums, & all the muddy roads lead
to parochial cul-de-sacs. The boats bow their heads
bayside. *Look at his hair!* the priest tells reporters,
his smile like a river of blood reflecting a man who rides
his horse toward a maelstrom of unanswered litanies.
Slaves' backs erected the temples in which we canonize
the spit of despots, pray for the lineage of the tormentor.
Father lent me new skin where there was none. We shout miracle,
wrap our bliss in lexicon. The white perjury speaks in us.

[INTRODUCTORY RITES]

Everywhere in Latin America: robe-engulfed children.
      We are told our angels are not worth grieving

over. A boy wanted to flee his body & became
      a rivulet of eyeless faces. Leftover, dysfunctional

prayer, when did he cease squealing to remember
      appellation? In Pittsburgh, a priest found guilty

of raping Honduran schoolboys. Bells blare mudslides.
      The poor are the last to receive communion.

Archdiocesan smoke rolling in a daze. In his hard drive,
      image after unfamiliar image of bewilderment.

*Everywhere is war. Everywhere is war. War in the east. War
      in the west.* Once, a child returned to his father,

but there was no father. A mother's arms sewn to her lap,
      broom heaving on the wall. Piety booms:

It's a conspiracy against God!—because God sits on His throne
      pondering downfalls He can't master, conundrums

He can't crack. The neighbors watch each other's children
      disappear into unmarked graves, mouths struck

with shoveled sermon. Tours between colonized motherlands.
      Children offered American chocolate, dollars—

what we grew up dubbing freedom & salvation when we were
      not yet honeycombed. A boy brushes his hair

as the alb falls on his black pants like a pallid whisper. When
      our waists were firmer than the crosses in their eyes,

we'd shine like newly jeweled candlesticks. They'd say, *No one*
    understands you. Only we do. There are incalculable

ways to dent a cross upon the body. Hail the hollowed bone.
    Hail the glorified extraction. Repent for missing grace.

[silence]

[LITURGY OF THE WORD: A CENTO]

I wrecked the bedroom   closer to the sea—   I've been dead for twenty years

Too many mouths open   The priest just said it   (a hawk on his arm)

These are dangerous days   We were so young then   Nighttime or morning

I am not like I was before—   these hands are sticky   In the backyard

the worm has laid eggs   stolen from our very eyes   You tell us not to sing

after Sunday   I will carry with me   my apple tree   We did

what was right   Three babies   jump in the river   in somebody's office

[LITURGY OF THE EUCHARIST]

If I whisper one of their names the Byzantine ghost
on the window might burst. A mother irons her son's
white shirt. The creases interminable. Compasses drunk
on direction. Sheep with slaughter trapped in their throats.
She splashes dirty water on deathbeds-to-be, inconsistent
confessional, battleground with burning orthodox doors
to nominate the muted combatant. O, sympathetic traitor.
We doom song on Sunday, bury blame under our mattresses
on Wednesday. We keep our savings & the hush-it money
stitched to our cushion covers. No space to bury
his torment. Who am I but a glimpse into avoidance, empty
outline of worship? Congregation of postperturbance.
I find myself pronouncing the scores of names in the torrents.

[silence]

[CONCLUDING RITE]

a running   absent of movement   history for a freshly
        cut curl   heaving sky   one half for an undernourished
child   the other to doggie bag   to a sick mother   a brother's
        skin train tracks at the border   crows behind their shack
floating in a high-church hush   elegy a father   won't care
        to translate   little brown arms folded into papier-
mâché   mud bricks   in the sacristy a man *past thirty*   *no beauty*
        at all   save for the ebullience   in his supplication expecting
a child's sparrow eyes   an incredulous belted father   sobbing
        like a wind with no intention   to halt   my mother
once said *some things*   *about your life*   *I'd rather not know*   fruit
        flies of burgundy silk wings on guava trees   the tongue
of shame the depth of rumor   shrouding the rooftops   coiling
        to the ground to plant multi-holed seeds   *I watch their spilt*
tears cloud & dull to pearl midair   the fumes of incensed
        innocence from a clay stove   *in a birth-drowse*   the wick-
child bodies between their fingers   our *fingers taken in by their own*
        haloes   how long until mourning is forgotten   like a rock
in the thunderous waters   of denial   fed & fed   to fresh mouths

MARROW

Then a wealthy Israeli student with a modeling career
& a military history invites us broke émigrés
to his apartment for drinks, our black shirts unbuttoned
in thirty-degree weather, with a strange fatigue
from dancing to M.I.A.'s *galang a lang a lang lang*
our bodies piled on the dorm room couch like raccoons
from an outtake of Fellini's *Satyricon*, minus the garlands,
minus the sugar daddies, minus the staged processions,
except processions are my forte, because I'm called
out for dressing like an aimless widow every summer,
deplumed messiah, & when another guest, the underage
daughter of a conservative politician from California
turns to me & says she can't find me attractive because
I'm Latino, what of the clinical light in the kitchen, what
of the lazy glow of the sci-fi helmeted lamps in the living
room, cartoonish but instinctively *Ma nuit chez Maud*,
the mariner's despair, how silence is the outside world
wanting to barge back in & claim the dispossessed body,
the body tousled on the stained carpet, to then taking
courses on Milton's divorce treatises, on binaries, on anti-
poetry, on mea culpas, postmodern Hail Marys, & how
I'd been told that following the Fall we grew proficient
at finding each other naked everywhere, in the nascent
bones of a fawn, in the wilderness of my brown skin,
in the voice boxes of tree trunks, because I'm always leaving
countries behind or maybe I can't get rid of my *For Rent*
signs decisively, & how the Fall is maybe symbolic
for how deep we'll burrow within us to still blame ourselves
for holding the map of rejection, that map with subjugated
creases, see Fig. 1 for assemblage, see Fig. 2 for the leper
who cries for clemency in the metaphor, where I worry
for the bones of the misfits who roam in the sewage system
beneath the tombs of my future fathers, their perilous dicks,
the Tacomas, the Kodachromes, the paintbrushes,
because it takes a mind of calcification to receive the grace
of that radiant refugee in the sky that's always intended
to touch us *Here is my heavenly handle, Here are my salt-
wounded arms*, for what decides to live outside of absence
but the thing that dreams of intangible rooms, & my savior,
he'll sit at the table, promising more than the allegory.

WHEN A PERSON SAYS GO BACK TO YOUR COUNTRY

that's exactly what you do, though you can't tell if you'll aggressively run or trip on national borders you'll have to make up for, the declaration so thunderous that even the floor can't hold still. & whether or not you have a passport on you or you're wearing any shoes at all to cross the thorniest distance of yourself, where oceans mean the same as potable water, or if the neighbors are having sex while you're dragging sacks of regrets that might as well be trash bags, leaky & heavy so they call the cops anyway, is insignificant. Because by then you're not an adult but a child aspiring to behave like a breadwinner, & when you can't find this country to which you're asked to return, though *back* has always meant finding an undisclosed space to vanish in, you try to give a retort. Not an argument, exactly, but a glimpse of the other body that can easily escape through our tongues. & you usually wait until the speaker has remembered to go back to *his* family, since his family *can* be remembered, & you curl into the night's sash, cold out of habit, to your dwelling, though there's nothing in there, even if you have purchased all the furnishings. Because a man who decides that a country is not an extension of one's heart can easily say that's not what he meant, that what he meant was more like *We all just need to get along, man. I don't want any trouble, man, I don't want any trouble.* & that's what you're debating when you remember that the child you carry on your back hasn't been fed in days, months, his heavy breathing a river overflowing, as you multiply uncertainty before you, which hides behind the safest sanctuaries, even inside. Most countries can't recall their mothers, just as shame can't be extracted with any medical devices, or prayers. If innocence can be taken by force only once, what is truly seized thereafter is absence, only absence.

RESTORED MURAL FOR ORLANDO

Seconds before the shooter sprays bullets on my brothers' & sisters'
bodies / the DJ stops the record from spinning / & I am interested

in that brief dazzle of pink light / how it spreads on iron-pressed
shirts until they turn purple / how a gun is a heart that has forgotten

to sing. The rapture in a stranger's eyes / a candid take on resurrection.
You visit Orlando to fantasize about the childhood you didn't have /

even though I grew up in Florida the trip was a luxury because I grew
up poor / & when I finally could afford it I took my parents to Universal

Studios / this is the first time I ever saw my mother get on a roller coaster
because she's always been ashamed of her weight & we ended up

buying a timeshare by mistake / not really by mistake / but by my illusion
that my parents worked themselves sick in the US so they needed

vacations / & the debt collectors still call us after all these years to remind
us of the Great Recession where my mother lost her job & my father

had to go into early retirement. Our mothers gave us names
so we would know what goes at the head of a tombstone / bare précis /

& our duty is to feel the isolation that any alignment of letters can trigger
when they're carved out of grief / since most of us were born or bloomed

out of sorrow like swans always bent on pond water or unpaid bills /
as though we were fishing for clues about our graves / or where we'll stop

to mislay our moisture on others' necks. & just the night before I went
out for Drag Night at Lush with four other poets / one reason to escape

my schedule & relive my adolescence / I am afraid of attending places
that celebrate our bodies because that's also where our bodies

have been cancelled / when you're brown & gay you're always dying
twice / I got to see thirteen performances by amateurs / a few special guests /

one queen who happened to make a stop in Minneapolis / she's a national
sensation / & the MC sang a raspy but virtuosic version of "When You're

Good to Mama" & the boys & girls & femmes lined up with their dollar bills /
which the queens scarfed down with their perfect bosoms & their teeth

& I turned to Danez & said the whole performance reminded me
of receiving communion as a child / how for me a church is a roof

that's always collapsing / though I might have been talking about
lovers paying their condolences / so often we forget that what kills us now

once believed in our survival / that a pistol & a rifle pulled apart
can be the shape of your arms as you pull a lover closer / that when his

teeth are black it means you picked the right bottle of Sauvignon /
that in our video games one can ride a bullet toward eternity.

* * *

My partner is asked to sing at the vigil in Loring Park. His choir
has commissioned an hour-long piece inspired by David Levithan's

Two Boys Kissing / in which a pair of teenagers participate in a kissing
marathon to set a new Guinness World Record. A Greek chorus of souls /

who won't be vanquished by the epidemic / find comfort narrating the tragic
but true events. *How can I sing for an entire hour about that much grief*

without breaking down during the performance? my partner asks me
as I scroll through the news. On the phone / my mother says the shooter's

hatred sprung from watching two men kiss in Bayside Marketplace in
the heart of Miami / & I am imagining how my mother might never approve

of me pressing my lips against another man's without that man being
my father or a mistranslation of him / because even our fathers have prayed

at least once for us to be gone / *No eres mi hijo maricón.* In Bayside
I held an old lover's hand before I moved away to college / the moon upon

the water like a wound that wouldn't heal / & he dumped me soon after /
said he couldn't bear the pain of me parting / which when you're older

you rank as necessary pain that trained you when to open up & shut
like a house with only hurricanes moving through it / or hasty promises.

Orlando like an orange / now green with mold / but still edible for some.
The evening of the shootings / after dinner with friends who grieve

by not dying / I come home to touch my partner's sweltering body /
a humid June evening without AC in Minnesota / far from the carnage

but still close to feel it / & we produce baby noises / an *uhn* for witness /
an *uhn* for hope / as we give shape to the carefree child of vulnerability

that runs between us every evening / safe but somehow lost / until my lover
falls asleep & I stay awake out of need & continue to whisper their names

as they are added to the list / like faces from a river of baptism. I forgive
the earth for not turning its neck further / for not allowing those pink lights

to keep flashing / for the cackles to remain intact no matter how boisterous.
In those seconds when their skin has never beamed so bright / so self-

assured / the bartender is shaking a piña colada / goose bumps flower
on someone's arms / the streets are humming from delight / a pair of lovers

walks in / another eagerly awaits the last call of the evening. It would seem
the record wants to keep spinning while we wipe their blood from the floor.

For them we learn to touch again. For them we walk home / & we are safe.

QUEERODACTYL

What we momentarily dubbed permission
was fiery ocean-wrapped crag, toeless oath.
This was our death dance, a slight whirlwind
that softened my tail with the VapoRub pulse,
nasty knots that wouldn't obliviate. & I raised
my ugliness elsewhere, disciplined the vestigial
slender-headed cluck-clucks. So much of finality
galloped to lodge to our fingers that we almost
mistook second silver-blinding coda for rest stop,
unwarranted hip shake for cherubic purpura.
Our skin agonized black radiation. The first time
he clutched my tail to pasture, I lifted his meat
castle, guided his hands, scorch-steady, like tea
leaves of ash, towards that aura within me that
once flamed my dog bones to mosh. Two suns
snapped, rose to fill my nostrils. Crazy what intimacy
will forge from colonized hunger: a map forever
extinguishing, taking more than a blitzed glitch
to cover the stratosphere. I almost evolved in cinders.

QUINCEAÑERA

para todas

After they dropped their machetes / on a christened orchard / my head rolled like a deflated ball de futból / & I mouthed the piss / -soaked muck / the blood that stung my prude reputation / leaving a riverbank of useless clues under my fingernails / leaf limbs / distressed dirt / My age matched another shallow grave / not the musky vestiary they threw me in / which they kept pressing over & over with their shovels / as a sign that had they suspected / they would have hanged my assailants by the balls / (I know / balls / now) / The rakers labored for hours / girls gossiped in their navy uniform skirts / on their way home from la prepa / boys eulogized their fathers tilling my corpse / a neighborhood crush found my fly-buzzing crown / a chunk of torso / expendable limbs / toddlers pretended to dig the ground / like little Chihuahuas swimming in sullied water / When you go missing inside these untransferable shrubs / they make you skip the morgue / Abuela's albatross / your mother forgets how to howl / in her own body / your father calls for dinner with the tone of a hot stove / Later / I took a gander at the Wall of Tears / where they place skeleton flowers / where they post our naïve portraitures / I had come back extracted / half ripped & naked / my lips kissing my own belly / inside a black garbage bag / a trick a teenager can only dream of performing / in front of her future absentees / What talents are we brown girls missing out on / before we can headline Broadway musicals / penned by lyricists familiarized with the weeded notes of ditches / appear in the front pages of American daily news / grace a constellation of highway ads in the arms of a heavily trafficked boulevard / muster men to stare at us from their automobiles / as they drive to their sizeable suburban homes / where they'll kiss their daughters goodnight / laboring over their curly shampooed hairs / the letters of their names framed in golden ostentation over their beds / their fathers' whispers retreating their lips / knowing when to drift home / while I'm stuck demonstrating how frontiers eat / the body / like small gazelles in an empty shopping mall / even I / a remorse / can't afford to walk into

QUEERODACTYL

Neither gag reflex nor shrill discouraged gravity.
Night could chugalug the kind of pulse that hounds
for shelter outside the melted, muscular zip code—

& don't angels plummet before they're privatized
under the Aristotelian method, the stress of what
you'll wear when Death proposes, sass & pizazz

of a surf swum right? A phallic light stripteasing
to conquer will tug at the throat for subservience
until language milks the Band-Aid of an echo.

To shed one's skin was to unmask his fraudulence,
thing of chickenhearted rock presuming wreathed
titanium. We renamed all things to delay their expiration.

Etymology declined to residue. Wasn't it in the coverage
of fire that we turned most introspective? *What I could've
done to an entire generation. Nothing is as explosive as refuge.*

Ever since I fell hostage to language I had expected
this death-in-minor to disciple the peeping unfanboys
of my modern arthritis. It's as if someone lit a match

to evaluate their loyalty to process over fair-waged traffic.
I never signed up to cardinal the rhumba, but gradually
my ultimatums shied around his cutter as he sulfured.

AFTER THE TEMPEST

As if to give up counting the slew of brown bodies
floating with their eyes wielded to the sky—because
we have trained in at least one position when dying,

though we disguise inheriting any knowledge of such
travesties—the guava trees abandon their bridal veils
in the branches of those who firmly believe dwelling

is carried under the skin, not in the limbs of what can flee.
& for a moment, his face crosses her face, their hands
fractured by the planks—or you can say recovery springs

from slaughter. Time in exodus: the bone-horticulture
under the swirling cloak of death . . .
                                        —How is this not
about the dissolution of friendship, the migratory birds

passing through the neo-necropolis? If we are mostly
displaced water—staggered, vigilant—when we drown
we are asking the flood tides to be gentler as we pray

away insufficiency. We, too, will drink to vanity. If only
I could trill in the range of loss without forgetting the angst
in my body—where the clouds coalesce around the ditch

to rename it rain, while the dried blood they call desire.

FINDING LOGIC IN A CRUSHED HEAD

para Pilingo

It is not a fallacy that the pulpería owner who wakes up
dressed in a tunic of warriors' pelos, or the milkman

pressing his rough hands against the cow's tectonic body,
remembers the skirted boy with ovarian lipstick for a tongue,

the boy who offered a tenth of his knees to the teeth
of a country with dentures. Because I have lifted my legs

to examine what birds will leave in abandoned nests. Because
I have lifted my hands from the chests of shipwrecked

men who've turned the seas into inconsolable lovers with
a misguided orgasm. Or perhaps the pulpería owner—

skin brown & preternatural as an Arizona bark
scorpion on sawdust—will stop laughing one day at the boy

who, before Death settled upon his ashy limbs
& his elbows were strangulated by exile's amplitude,

helped me capture those polysyllabic butterflies one pins
before nightfall. The boy's fine head rested on the tracks

before the train trampled it like masa mix rolled with an aunt's
hands on an oven, as he tried to cantankerize the border.

Moths stuck to the dictionary of the pulpería slimeball's
mouth, as an ulcered sun rose from his dry lips. Divinatory

wings in the rusted nail geometry of a bullet hole.
Our abuelas taught us to run like eyeless ghosts in a backyard.

My ancestors have crimpled wooden doors with their hands,
the men have, & there is no remedio for the hummingbirds

a mother casts from a mouth agape, the tongues gone missing—
those witnesses of railroads, carnations for the wounded.

A new truth flits among flame anisacanthus, aquilegia,
firebush, angel's-trumpets. My vacancies know boundless

absence. I have seen the eyes of hummingbirds blink backwards,
when direction was once read as a declaration for agency. &

yet few milkmen know how the wretched live off spoilage.
Ask me where to find need. I am ringmaster of my own sinkings.

JURISDICTION

On the contrary: ghosts do aspire to bring
the living to trial—chomp their passports
with Olympian chasms—as when one
harpsichords a stallion to libate

from the palms of forgetting—moonlight
shoveling out tongues from a slivered carafe,
the land cursed congruence, the land punta
dance rocketed at the unyielding empires.

* * *

Justice denounces the sun for displaying
humble horrors, bleeds amendments
from her blindfolds. A blip of boys—
nine-year-old regrets—trace with their eyes

the military man's gutting of his rifle.
Our country squats behind poisonous woods,
perches, as if on latrines—wrists tightened
with ropes of habit behind her silence.

* * *

Which death will eventually dawn on us?
Child of butchery, I now rove in nowheres,
skin aqueducts, oldfoundlands. I hide
my ambitions in skunk-stamped burrows,

pluck sarcophagi out of city diapers—
I let the rain stone me, knowing full well
my futile desire to belong. One day I was
a house. The next I exhausted all the tenants.

THOSE SEVENTY-TWO BODIES BELONG TO US

para Luis

You novelize a route with flesh dumped at the ranch, can't backtrack
the courage of miles we traversed in the dark, on a sighing speedboat,

through jungles that spat only shoes, calzones, bodies twisted
like guitarras when there's no grito left in them to pluck. Back home,

we priested our mornings with sun-dried sombreros, communed
with our ghosts & had no wish to sacrifice our bellies, our terneros,

our Consuelos. With wings from acero, we'd crash latitudinal objections,
mystify Bengay on the mouths of our map-torn feet, pay no heed

to grief's ambidextrous strophes. If we choked on our own blood
we harpooned optimism. But when the vans deadlocked our pilgrimage

we knew our shadows had crumbed the anesthetic vultures.
They pressed their loaded beaks upon our backs until our knees bent

sour orange. One asked if we served the enemy, but we took enemy
to mean a seed that sits quietly underfoot, abashed to vestibule

the grating sun. Blindfolded, we faced the gloom volcanoes
of their mothers. How those mothers might've screamed like ours

in their tortured independence: bloody thunder in the brown-starched
symphonies, a wind that howled & shoved its thumbs through feral lands

probing for judgment or commiseration. Chingado god that copycatted
these legs from monotony. Chingado god that hewed our wrists,

a pair of stems to strap behind our wrested boots & jeans. Whoever
supplied a plea to that deviant afternoon's rationed blessings

neglected to add chile, sazón, a nosegay of tortillas to the long road.
Mothers who've come to reclaim our tongues in the dirt: remind us

of the braids in the phrasings of our dreams before we vanished. Pat
the ground for the bodkinned orchids. Wasn't it yesterday we were

siphoning forecasts with our fingers roving on the table? Or caught
your chests pain leavened & stilled them with the rumpus of our hopes?

QUEERODACTYL

    My heart was a dystopian
berry budding in water tiger

lilies claiming
      hocus-pocus wonder. I was broken

vanity, vixen vase, victorious tête-

à-tête—the Scrabble game nobody won
      because the tiles aspired speculums.

Ocean-misaligned brook / brook-misaligned
                    agua

—where else could these gospels have dawned
if not in the bellies of men

hyenaing a becoming?

            Twerking in church,

I outperformed the candles
diarized in the simpleminded annexation.   Wussup,

      Blastoise
with the veiniest homebound
            pika-pika aim?

Wussup, Sims
      Chumbawamba Family Portrait Simulation?

        St. Sunny of the Sissies
beheld the bukkake throng

           of mojo-coated cartilage
squandered
    on the refurbished bunk

for new cetaceans. A dazzling jeremiad
　　　shone me dead

until I gridlocked the algebraic expressions
　　　of my body in question marks.

　　　　　　These syndicated fiyahs
stigmatized my herculean magma
　　　　　　　　　shades,

　　　but I held these walls apart,
every inch of my mascara cut off
　　　　　　　apple pie.

　　You watched me hobble home
while the streets coalesced magenta. Tell Momma

　　　the holes I cover with one error

swell—& there are only inadvertent landscapes
　　　　　to dollop with nonetheless.

SELF-PORTRAIT ACCORDING TO GEORGE W. BUSH

In May 2006, Bush addressed a televised speech to the American public &
Congress, pressing for stricter immigration laws. Language from that speech
appears here.

[PINTURA/BLOOD]

   Scent of fried flesh rolling over cracked white paint
   as a young waitress, una
   mejicana my age,
wipes the ketchup bottles with a coarse rag that resembles a bib.

           I don't ask for her name

but I know she keeps an infant in one corner of the restaurant
where the patrons can't see it—day laborers, construction

workers—the prophet can be found anywhere, you see:
       en la grieta, en el grito, in the knife

of the butcher in the kitchen, in the depluming
        of the white lilies.

[ACEITES/WATERBOARDING]

For decades,

the Angel of Death says,

the United States has not been in complete
control of its borders . . . border as in

marca de zapatos de Payless for which I got a bloody

nose at school,

inner city cymbals, halfway house doors,
la marca de la bestia in my queer vestiary, the brothel-home

where Mickey fucked us all, the immigrant's *Funeral*

March,

la mancha de mi país, el maricón who can't stop sweeping
roads with his tongue.

[REPRODUCCIONES/MELTING POT]

We will construct high-tech fences
in urban corridors, he says, como Dolphin Mall, como

Westland Mall en Hialeah, como Valsan—donde los que vienen
son mummified—to *build new patrol roads,*
                                        undetectable barbed
wire wound like colmillos on a clothesline
tied from one immigrant's feet

                        to another's, factories
where shame can be manufactured into appliances we can't afford,
where flesh billows the soul of a dream.

[MODELO/SURVEILLANCE SYSTEM]

The baby's father has left the produce of his exile.

& she winks at me every time my parents stare at the dusty pictures
of players de futból on the wall, los machos
lionized. The owner
                    is Chinese Venezuelan American
& has memorized our order—so that the hole in the wall
                    momentarily becomes our home in the wall.

The waitress excuses herself, as we conspire
by not acknowledging where the child's cries

                    come from. *Illegal immigrants live
                    in the shadows of our society*, La Muerte says,

but what can the voice learn from its echo
once the pronouncement has left the mouth?

[ACUARELAS/DDT POWDER]

The Texan uses verbs like *sneak* & insults like *criminals*

stayed	*broken*
verify	*beyond the reach*
enforce	*& protection of*
shut	*the American law*
secure	*debate*
apprehend	*human smugglers*
detain	*drug dealers*
catch	*risk*
confront	*terrorists*
discourage	*illegal immigrant*
assimilate	*burden*
deport	*"our friend"* —& yet

the deported will always forget to pack the second ghost
she never meant to give birth to, in a country
that now hates her—a ghost with which we must learn to cohabit,

> inhabit, let it possess our bones
> because that is what shame does
> with fence material.

For us, departure

will always signify the return to the unknown
language of *our neighbor* when he's gone.

[LUZ/BORDER PATROL]

On TV
        the mothers who look like mine, perhaps a little
lighter around the neck, wearing aviators, their faces
        sunburnt as they swear their allegiance to the cause:
help raid
        undocumented visionaries. The cameraman tries
to keep up with the one who moves like a tornado,
        as confident as anyone who's never faced
deportation.
        I turn to my parents, their silence bending in a cell.
Let's forget
        this woman's nationality for a minute. Let's say,
as an old roommate used to maintain, that all Latinos
        are to be loved because y'all are so warm—
perhaps because he's never
        known how some of us will bundle our fears
like do-rags over our heads, to cross a river that pummels
        like monochrome armies over our sovereignty.
The one time I've run
        with my demons packed in the trunk of a car
was when I volunteered
        at a nursing home & my parents found out
I'd fallen for a boy's lips. High school existentialism.
        The boy had to sneak out when his parents
weren't home
        so he could call me from a payphone; from my end,
I had to keep my parents' English knowledge at a minimum.
        Years later, that woman has moved in between
the channels. A ghost
        that mistakenly thinks the shamed body is the only
home she can know.
        She walks beside you like a tributary of penance.
As when I learned that you can love without the pretense
        of death, from anonymous men who would bite
hard into my nipples
        before they could spit out pubic hair. A wise friend
once said that a hen will almost always lose a chick

on her way to the nail salon. The chick
will never kill
    his own brother, toss his body in a river, wait
until he hears
    about the crime from a stranger's facsimiled mouth.
Water levels rise like severed hands over the world's borders.
    Make no mistake that you will, in the humdrum,
forget what has haunted you.
    Then, one day, a sparrow will crack open the valves.
Bodies will swim under the furniture, on your neighbors'
    porch. The greenest ferns. & you will be there
alone to receive them—
                    not a part of your history spared.

[COLORES/DRONES]

BBQ Spare Ribs (5) costillas barbeque (5) 7.25
Estás caught otra vez entre qué comer today & the rest of the week because you've started seeing a gastroenterologist & he's said we've got to be careful about your colon because it's inflamed. Te recuerdas

Wonton Soup sopa de mariposas 2.00/3.00
of all the MSG you consumed in college, from that place with the bubble tea que creo qu'is closed by now? They took away the Pizza Hut, left un McDonald's. Some wounds nunca se abandonan tan easy. El frío

Hot & Sour Soup sopa picante y agria 4.00
of those Hyde Park streets nunca went away, as an extension of the art project you ended up embodying, pero which you can't comprehend because you're always living outside of it. Like a breeze en una bandera

Special Fried Rice especial de la casa. 5.50/7.75/16.25
que se dobla y se dobla or a house que reza todas las noches for you not to come back. Because la lengua del immigrant can wrap any leftovers, palos de guayaba, pistas de aviones, el cura que nunca pudo bless you.

Chop Suey Chicken con pollo 6.00/7.75
& when you got a tu dorm, tu roommate te dice que his Russian is as rich as Chekhov's, but he's not interested in the stories of possession you carry en tu pecho de pelos que se enredan into huts para los que se escapan.

Chicken Lo Mein tallarines con pollo 6.00/8.50
You drive past los Home Depots, los restaurantes hondureños, y te entra una tristeza to know that what connects you to your community is suspicion, regret, el why didn't I go to school, el why you've been so lucky

Chicken w. Broccoli pollo con brócoli 6.00/8.00
que your parents never forced you to get a job, you could concentrate on your materias, where would we be if we'd been given the same opportunities you've had, although yo vivo in a house where I'm waiting

Shrimp w. Lobster Sauce camarones con salsa de langosta 6.50/9.50
for the master to return. I'm a wounded canino, can't you tell? Barking at myself for
not barking at the forms of trees. Tantos knots en la garganta como en los zapatos one
can't stop to loosen because one has to return

Sweet & Sour Chicken pollo agridulce 6.00/9.00
to work o te va a despedir el patrón. Tu madre begs you to stop spending your money
en chucherías, en going out con la otra gente de dinero, that's not why you left Miami,
that's not why she's detonating bombs on her back.

Soda refrescos 1.00
But what she doesn't know is that loneliness is a symptom one becomes so adept at
concretizing in a foreign land, en el país de las manos rajadas,
where you eat a meal cooked by someone who has a similar story de huesos.

[SOMBRAS/DETENTION FACILITY]

A Chinese restaurant owner in Novi, Michigan,
houses five undocumented workers from Mexico
in the basement of his residence. Wages under
a clean bathtub. Every meal stirred by silence.
Their ages: 16, 18, 18, 23 & 23 to demonstrate
that death likes to show off in odds & pairs.
The fire begins as an unheard prayer over an old
mattress & spreads like wild deer once it is heard.
Think of church bells, the end of recess. No fire
extinguisher, no smoke alarm to beep for consolation.
We think that everything that burns was meant to be
consumed first. Food instead of injustice. Water
instead of intolerance. Imagine the flames spreading
like una sad niña learning to make her first bed,
pressing her palms against a bed that won't be hers.
The smoke in her hair crawling over the walls.
She proceeds to grab a copy of the Bible in every
language, since Bible is one of men's primal screams.
If I had to gather those words I've christened
on disaffected ears, all the missing accents
de mi español, I wouldn't have to fear going
back to the country of papier-mâché. America,
when will you stop transiting over the ashes
of our tongues? English is just another word
for deathbed. Once, as a child, I remember running
into my grandmother's house. Someone had set
the house of las maricas on fire. The tin roof
caved in. I burned in the brown skin's apathy.

[FONDO/CRIMINAL BACKGROUND CHECK]

. . . we will employ motion sensors . . .
> we linger under these highways of empty rhetoric

like intersections that can't be seen no matter how wide the wings
. . . infrared cameras . . . unmanned aerial vehicles . . .

. . . to prevent illegal crossings . . .
> our concrete arms are burned from working

entire gospels' worth under the sun. or running from fumes
. . . the guard will assist the border patrol by operating

surveillance systems . . . analyzing intelligence . . . installing
> in the bathroom—what a horrible joke it is to unlearn

breathing. to hold your nose, after all, because once you existed
fences & vehicle barriers . . . building patrol roads . . .

. . . providing training . . .
> to yourself. never to them. remember when you unlearned

to walk with your own feet, to speak with your own mouth.
. . . for many years the government did not have

enough space in our detention facilities to hold them
> that also happened to you? how well we remember

the dates when our dignity was taken from us, the sunlight spilling
while the legal process unfolded . . .

. . . they walk across miles of desert in the summer heat
> over the stove, the back of every house your house.

walter benjamin developed the concept of the angel of history
or hide in the back of eighteen-wheelers to reach our country . . .

. . . this creates enormous pressure on our border that walls
> after observing paul klee's painting *angelus novus*.

this is how i see it: el ángel gabriel got stuck working
& patrols alone will not stop . . . a key part of that system

should be a new identification card for every legal
      an extra shift. on his way to our barrio he got caught up

smelling los pastelitos de piña, which, because of his holy senses,
foreign worker . . . this card should use biometric technology

such as digital fingerprints to make it tamperproof . . .
      still smelled fresh, though they'd been sitting there all day.

la migra shows up & gaby can measure destruction
. . . I believe that illegal immigrants who have roots in our country

& want to stay should have to pay a meaningful penalty
      only after it's happened. he sees the waitress's quiet trailer

& thinks there's nothing to see. angels work in extremes.
for breaking the law . . . to pay their taxes . . . to learn english . . .

& to work in a job for a number of years . . . english is also
      hermanos, hermanas, niños, niñas are apprehended,

but the angel is mystified by the flashing lights, since heaven
the key to unlocking the opportunity of america . . . english

allows newcomers to go from picking crops to opening
      shines brightly from its never-ending stupor of contentment.

one apartment's lights won't turn on the same way. a new
a grocery . . . from cleaning offices to running offices . . .

from a life of low-paying jobs to a diploma . . . a career . . .
      story will move in without a care for backstory. the poet

will need to carve another name on his
& a home of their own . . . arms. the ghosts are out there, shoveling.

MARERO

I learned to cleave through the whirlwinds on his back
                              —unclaimed lacerations,
bullet holes gaping
                  on forsaken walls. Mercy
                          tattoos. He blew ships
                                    of crystal meth in my ear—
the sea, a nightmare
in gunmetal gown. He said
               My ass so tight baby—a murmur
                    of splinters
                           half-birthed on bruised muscle.
        On his shaved head,
black horses
            in a long funeral procession of ashes.
                                    & from his shoulders,
names in calligraphy
                  of the missing,
                                 the dead
shoveling their pulperías
from the ground,
                where their sons
                            & daughters still dream
                of having mouths. I hung
my coniferous body
from his nipple rings,
                               ducking the coral snake
                                   coiling
down his gravel chest—
            a girl with the tail of a dragon
                     sucking on a headless girl on his bicep,
mouthing
Corre cabrón.

                                      Corre—
a prisoner, like me, to a body
our mothers have placed
                       inside garbage bags, old jokes—
                               the dirt under
his nails, fertile.
On his thighs, yucca petals. In his shade,

                                                  a communion of spare sweat.
                                   If I licked the word *SUR* on his neck,

I found the ala.
If I licked *NORTE*
                on the scruff of his neck,

                                                  a juncture where feathers
                                                      became carnations.

Again & again he pressed
his lit cigarette on my knees & asked

                                                  to guess where his first scar
                                                          would emerge—

how the headmasters teach us brown boys
to shed our inheritance,

                                                  drink from the current wine.
                                                  Once, while the rosary

beads about my neck
                ripened like lesions,

                                                  he ripped my tongue,

spat out a lizard.
                That night I bled

                                                  in his hands, & from his hands

a seagull cawed
at the wrong bestial father.

                                                  Armpit: torn banner. Love:
                                                          desert gnats.

Whenever I've spilled deliverance

                                                  down the shallow throats
                                                      of unbelievers,

I've meant for loss
to be drunk. For thumbs to frame new eyes.
                The wood storks

                                                  return to their swamps

& our groins
        praise all that's been banished.

QUEERODACTYL

With droopy but *WORK IT GIRL* wings, Queerodactrix

couldn't find the restroom amidst all that burning
sulfur in the air, a mirror of soot on the dance floor

to gaze at the unknown, though the unknown

was passé. They say dead languages roam in those
who linger during after-hours, but I'm still keeping count

of the burials our mothers never had because death

is also an unsent love letter. When the ground
erupted under toothless seas, our ecosystems were

preparing for the real masquerade ball, absolving a dream

whose beginning had gone missing, requiring expertise
in misplacement. The holiest of beds I've laid in

have had my own reflection to crush & console.

The first time our planet went numb with melancholy,
Versadactyl, learned in the art of flying with a limp

& strut, couldn't match the order of the Mayan calendar.

Our storytellers tell us that lizards fell like Babylons
under the Viral Inquisition. That the groin

of a dream tasted sweeter when guzzled from above

before it poisoned even the shadows,
always the last to die. Let's say that what results from

abandonment is also miraculous. Even when the

fairy-angels couldn't rummage for food, they still had
their own instincts for sustenance. I have seen children

hoard entire nations of giants for a peek at the night sky.

I have heard their giggles in my own solitude afterward.

MARROW

The two-hearted spirit-spider generates blood

portraitures out of lies
                            which in due course
                            mutate into forked

tongues in my mouth—those daggers

I'm too hesitant to brandish.

                            Poets often speak
                            of the residual pain

left behind when language has been fractured—

but how little we understand
where to mend the cartilage,
                            restitch our ghosts.

        Sarah: you are the mutant

        mutants are too ashamed to mention.

La Maricona.   La Pata.   La Bullet-Riddled

Puta—bystander of mauled angels,

                    one of those bastard superheroes

who owe the earth / nothing.

                    Your social worker writes down:

                    She demonstrates exemplary
                    movement of the Aristotelian
                    model: exposure,

rising shame, crown of thorns, bastardization—

the metaphysical resolution.

I fell in love with a man once

who was forced as a child to swallow his own

vomit when he couldn't eat anymore. *The failure*

of line breaks when some cuts   won't bleed.

Every evening,

                after sex, I could hear

the whirring of the blender:

                    bone
            prayer   prayer
        bone   bone
        prayer   prayer
            bone   bone
                prayer

                        Nothing has boundaries

in the ways I'm willing
to worship. Who cares for baptism

                when the body

is excess holiness   waiting to combust.

QUEERODACTYL

Woke up like strangulated terracotta   empress.   Woke up like
        measled fantasia sewage.   The goldmines are revamped.
We've defaulted on our loans.   Self-portrait as co-   opted ravine.
        Dish-washing roaches in mold.   This song has blown
piñatas, conga lines   of those disappeared.   Why won't you gob
        your empathy for this killing?   We believe in mortal
flight   & so our deaths are suspended,   obedient escalade.
        We rummage through Icarus's bravery as if we weren't ourselves
tumbling   through the meteorological chaos   of our ancestry.
        I have stared into the eyes   of someone with borrowed skin,
borrowed name,   servant to the wrong   verge of the river.
        She knotted her hair   to the strobe lights,   as gaffs passed
her body undeterred.   Later,   she smeared her gloom
        on the outside walls   of the earth.   Some will say
that is how history begat history.   I'll say
        glory to fate's incorrigible nature   & toward which
we violently stroll.

QUEERODACTYL

Spandex leggings authenticating my anaerobic
    exit strategies. Crotch but a bumper sticker
in a heretofore-fleeting waterloo. Crunk repentance. I span

our doomed alphabet soup like Jane Fonda's antiwar legs
    in callisthenic videos. My zenith of hair a brown,

       wannabe-Fawcett, mean-ole-toucan pupic papa—.
He who so feeds on an entire corpus & still
starves helms the colloquium outside the bathroom
of transubstantiation.
               Tonight—a vastly archived Nietzschean
nighttime—I anal bleach my humpty-

dumpty stigmatas.
    Boys conch with crimson Hollywood carpets that disentangle
from their cavities, accustoming their catwalks upon the blood
clots of their mamacitas. Like a mythic infantry, the thirsty

roaches begin to leatherflock. I plié before the gas
cloud lifting jumbo leaves. As twilight uncrowns
the shade,   I howl effluvium. Switchblade   hue to hue.

PAYDAY LOAN PHENOMENOLOGY

we sit in my stepfather's 2000 Nissan Altima with a broken

AC   me in the backseat   my parents in the front   of a pending storm

sweating   reciting our overused interior monologue   *this must be*

the last time we'll take out a loan   we'll have no use for future loans

Mom & I get two weeks to pay the loan   my stepfather a whole

month because he's retired   has five credit cards left to resolve   he

used one to come see me graduate   their first time in New England

& I place my hand on my mother's shoulder   I can feel the behemoth

of impotence stomping inside her   a familiar trespasser   if her anxiety

kicks in   her stomach upset   she falls from a cliff of *what if I hads*

like glowworms during nights when the Honduran government

coordinates a series of power outages   & we break tortillas

by the candlelight   drinking blowflies in the water

                        crushed ice is trapped in the AC's mouth   our sound

financial adviser   won't treat the air we breathe like a Ponzi scheme

which is to say that even after sixteen years   the car has less than 100,

000 miles   we run upwards of 100,000 miles in an average lifetime

within the corridors of our worst fears   as we seek some modicum

of salvation from there never being enough   & we ought to acknowledge

that more often   we ought to drive back to the beach & throw ourselves

in the water   anticipate the tropical storm always heading our way

you get a customized tropical storm where I was raised   & you watch

as a cruise ship sails beside you   how many times have I seen dissenters

board that melancholic ship   & wave from the deck of confusion

as though I carried an invisible heart   shaped camera

                                        my mother

is wearing a long-sleeved shirt   the sun is skating careless circles

on our necks   my mother might roll a towel over her arm   one day

I said in a psychoanalysis class that I had a dream about her

breastfeeding me   & handing me off to my aunt because I bit

off something that wasn't her nipple   in the car my stepfather

is hoping he'll find a decent hobby before he dies   he used to sail

boats back in Cuba   lost his possessions as the revolution gained traction

& I disappointed him when I showed no interest in fishing   my parents

do not believe in friendship since every apartment we move into is built

with unheard screams   night lamps thrown across the room with shades

of soft pink flowers   a jar of nacho cheese on the floor   my stepfather

slipping & almost   landing on the shards   of my mother's buckler

the payday loan shop

needs its own parking lot   we pull up in front of the crater where we

hired legal counselors to help us apply for green cards   how we have

a firm connection to the things that cause us trauma   is a story

worth retelling   our citizenship like a dry spell   operation florid

storm   social expendability   we carry blue passports everywhere we go

to remind us of how others have been snatched from their dreams

our skin callused from too much persecution   we don't live

in Arizona   so we are los afortunados   no longer like prohibited

liquor in a dusty one bedroom for two families   we are USDA approved

preprocessed   GPSd   our liberties red   white   & blue

police lights over a spillage of innocence   we are animals with eyes

shaped like prison cells   but we can't hold any more inmates

because our vision has been incarcerated   if we swim underwater

we can't decide when to rise   to draw another breath   from harm

& the cops here

are evidently Latinos   will batter you when they catch you hustling

but dance   with you during pride parades   which are more like funerals

their truncheons like limp bodies swinging   inconclusive   the white cops buying media luna sandwiches   sinking their teeth on what they

mispronounce with pride   the Black cops enjoying Latin music   *I know*

you want me   with my hands up   *you know I want cha*   legs

spread apart   my parents teach me that when you labor   tirelessly

God rewards you   but even Job knew that browns' faiths won't bring

back their dead   because we woke up this morning to face the mirror

of disconsolation beyond our eyelids   in nature there is an animal serving

as scapegoat for all living things   a memory that consumes

all others   I am that dollar bill greasy men must take spit

index & thumb   to pull apart

in some hell even a cash advance

stands for protection   as soon as the other customers begin to show up

my mother says we should hurry in   she shrinks the distance   of a

long & burdensome desert beneath her feet   & my stepfather worries

that his car might get towed   in *North by Northwest* Cary Grant

dodges a crop duster in an attempt to find the man with whom

his identity has been mistaken   the bullets hit the ground around him

& I remember when we used to hide from La Migra   I remember

making a carapace with my arms around my head when my *boicunt*

equaled deportation   so that *fag* was the only thing that could impale me

a man once neared his nose to my neck & said   *I can get used to*

you smelling like a child

& now a long line of people

has started to snake around the shop   people who look like us who sound

like us when they say gracias   confidence is our rare species

who yawn like us in the middle of a plead   & cross their arms

viejos with Styrofoam cups of coffee   who also cross themselves & scratch

their heads   grieve like us because our bones cry the same way

& when we ask to use the restroom   without a doubt the restroom

is broken   they haven't called the plumber   we acknowledge one
another   say *buenos días   cómo les va   usted es el siguiente   cuántos*
días tengo para pagar   no los hemos visto en meses (even though

we were there two months ago   skipped a month)   *the cash dispenser*
is broken   sign here & here   & here & put your initials here   & here
& here   don't forget to fill out this information right here   how is
your father   we haven't seen him around here much (he too was there

two months ago)

the same woman stamps one sheet   stamps another   she
is enjoying her new life as a mommy   couldn't take too many days off
after she had the baby   her husband was laid off   & the shop
is carpeted gray   you can tell where the café con leches have fallen

a woman needs to buzz you in   they don't see us like criminals
but nothing says we can't be   *no seas malpensa'o viejo   no sean*
malpensa'os   why must you think the worst about people

& you should see us in the car on our way home   looking like
we got paid   looking like we just went to physical therapy

shoulders back in place   no more sore necks   we'll pay the bills
on time   won't have any money leftover   my heart is a marathon
with no participants   my mother will ask my stepfather if he remembered
to take out the chicken from the freezer   leave it on the sink for dinner

there is a comfort to preparing a meal together   even if you won't
ever eat it   together

we get home   our door opens
to an apartment we can't accept we can't afford   it's closer to work

& we want to skip the morning traffic   our footsteps hit a floor
that's lost all sensation in its fingers   there's been so much rain lately

all our umbrellas can do is sink deeper   our furniture never belongs
to us   we are expecting its undetermined future owner to show up

& load it to the back of his truck   dinner will be served   tasting

a miracle requires disbelief we must steal from one another   we open

the fridge & a voice in our heads says everything in there   is a kind

of mercy   the light bulbs need replacing   in there an unfathomable

darkness   a stillness shows us how one replicates a body

just to practice disavowing it

as ritual   we count the time it takes us

to walk from our bedrooms to the living room   from the living room

to the bathroom   from the bathroom to the kitchen   a false sequence

a false geometry   most days nothing   can find us in that untamable

forest of dimensions   our minds can't listen to themselves when we

crawl away from each other's gaze   my mother a war zone   my father

a dismantled effigy for a country of fanatics   I was in high school

when my parents said we'd eat less that week so I could buy a book

I felt I needed to read   because it appeared on a list of texts you perused

to improve your verbal skills   I read it in one sitting   I remember

looking up when I was done   my stepfather fixed on the news

my mother storing leftovers   I didn't close the book until they both

fell asleep   afterward I understood why certain books are banned

why I distrust perception   why my parents praised walls so I didn't

have to see the abuse   or think in absolutes   that whoever claims

empathy   might be forging shackles for your ankles   somewhere

QUEERODACTYL

After they locate & excavate your wing fossils,
perseverance might be the trait you're known for.
How swiftly you sloped downward to pick up
the carcasses floating just above the bloodstained
surface of your old neighborhood. In the laboratory,
the paleontologists will use radiometric dating
to zoom into what bequeathed you that agency to fly.
This one might have outlasted all the others,
they'll say. *Might have even seen each one disappear
behind a bolt of fire blasted from who knows where.*
Or you might have been the first to vanish, directly in
the way of the asteroid's course. Who will, in the end,
exhume our myths conclusively? A young angel's bones,
shaped just like yours, were uncovered this morning.
A group of diggers hadn't found anything exciting
for months—in jeopardy of losing all their funding.
I, too, have buried myself under the heavy presence
of change, from a longing, perhaps, to find my remnants,
or their profiles, in places where curious strangers
might prize them. Church is anything with a pair
of wandering hands & a bucket. I, too, have questioned
the usefulness of finding a body stuck in a perpetual
position of near flight—arms extended like the incandescence
from a lamppost at night—& wished it be mine.

NOTE ON THE TITLE

In the mid-1800s, William Walker, an American filibuster, attempted to take over Central America and reimagine the region as slave states under United States rule. At first, he tried to build a colony in Mexico. After successfully taking advantage of civil unrest in Nicaragua, Walker became president of the country in 1856. With United States President Franklin Pierce's endorsement, he ruled for a year. During his reign, Walker went to war with Costa Rica and plagued the country with cholera. He was eventually defeated by Honduran General Florencio Xatruch's troops, which included Salvadorian soldiers. Walker was charged and executed in 1860. Because Xatruch's name was difficult to pronounce, as Nicaraguans welcomed the general and the soldiers, they yelled, *¡Aquí vienen los catruches!* From Xatruch's name, Salvadorians became known as salvatruchos, and Hondurans catrachos.

NOTES

"Catrachos" alludes to Cuban American artist Ana Mendieta's earth-body sculptoperformances.

"Queerodactyl (We vogued in graveyards, headstones big)" is after Patricia Smith.

"Queerodactyl (You don't have to watch me whip my wings)"—and other poems in this series—employs terms from voguing and paleontology. This poem alludes to the films *Mommie Dearest* (1981), *The Deer Hunter* (1978), *The Land Before Time* (1988), and *Paris Is Burning* (1990). The poem also alludes to the pornographic term *gay-for-pay*.

"Our Lady of Suyapa" refers to the Virgin of Suyapa, the equivalent of the Virgin Mary in Honduras. In the Marvel Universe, the Phoenix Force is frequently associated with the *X-Men* character Jean Grey.

"My Great-Grandmother's Egg Thief" alludes to Cantinflas, a Mexican icon in Latin American cinema. Cantinflas often used slapstick to portray peasants and working-class people on screen.

Pulperías appear in several poems; they connote general merchant stores, taverns, canteens, bodegas, liquor stores, and more. Most pulperías were originally found near mining sites. In 1578, Spanish settlers turned Tegucigalpa into a mining town.

"The American Dream" is after Philip Levine. Allapattah is the Seminole word for alligator.

"Allapattah Branch Library" alludes to the chupacabras, a creature found in Latin American folklore.

"Queerodactyl (Jewelry boom box spittin' *bidi bidi bom bom*)" interpolates its refrain from Queen of Tejanx music Selena Quintanilla-Pérez's song "Bidi Bidi Bom Bom." The poem also alludes to rapper Pitbull ("dales") and the Gospel of John (6:1–51).

"Arthur's Spelling Trubble" incorporates scenes and cites characters from *Arthur*, the animated educational TV series (1996–).

"Queerodactyl (Bones classified as those of a seafarer. Nimble)" is for Ryan Keith Skipper (1981–2007), killed in a hate crime in Wahneta, Florida.

The "Marrow" poems allude to the *X-Men* universe character Marrow, also known as Sarah. Marrow is a member of the Morlocks, a tribe of mutants considered outcasts even among mutants. Marrow's "powers" allow her to sprout bones from her body, which she can then brandish for self-defense.

"Amor Eterno" is for Walter Orlando Tróchez (1982–2009), Honduran political and LGBTIQ rights activist. This poem shares its title with Mexican singer Juan Gabriel's song.

Material for "In Service of Silence" comes from personal accounts and the following articles: "By the Numbers: The Catholic Church's Sex Abuse Scandals," *Vocativ*; "South America has become a safe haven for the Catholic Church's alleged child molesters. The Vatican has no comment," *PRI*; "Chilean church offices raided as part of sex abuse probe," the *Associated Press*; and "US Catholic Church reports big rise in sex-abuse allegations," the *Associated Press*. The poem also borrows lyrics from Bob Marley's song "War" and lines from Sylvia Plath's poem "Candles." The cento "Liturgy of the Word" is composed of lyrics from Sinéad O'Connor's albums *The Lion and the Cobra* (1987) and *I Do Not Want What I Haven't Got* (1990).

Between 2004 and 2014 approximately 3,400 cases of sexual abuse were referred to the Vatican on the grounds of their credibility. Between 2017 and 2018, over 1,400 additional allegations. Thousands remain unreported.

"Marrow (Then a wealthy Israeli student with a modeling career)" references Éric Rohmer's film *Ma nuit chez Maud* (1969).

"Restored Mural for Orlando" was written in memory of the victims of the 2016 Pulse nightclub massacre in Orlando, Florida. "When You're Good to Mama" is a song from the musical *Chicago*. The Danez in the poem is the poet Danez Smith.

"After the Tempest" was written for the victims of Hurricane Mitch. In 1998, the Category 5 hurricane formed in the Atlantic and left behind over 11,300 dead in Central America. The damage was so catastrophic that evidence of the hurricane can still be found throughout the region.

"Finding Logic in a Crushed Head" is after Diane Seuss.

"Those Seventy-Two Bodies Belong to Us" is after the 2010 San Fernando massacre.

"Queerodactyl (My heart was a dystopian)" alludes to the British alternative band Chumbawamba, the video game series *The Sims*, and Cuban mojo sauce.

Each subheading of "Self-Portrait According to George W. Bush" is an intentional mistranslation.

"Marero" refers to a gang member from Central America, particularly from El Salvador and Honduras.

"Queerodactyl (Woke up like strangulated terracotta)" was inspired by Beyoncé's song "***Flawless" (2013).

"Payday Loan Phenomenology" cites lyrics from rapper Pitbull's song "I Know You Want Me (Calle Ocho)" (2007).

"Queerodactyl (After they locate and excavate your wing-fossils)" is after Matthew Olzmann.

ACKNOWLEDGMENTS

Gracias to all the editors and hogares that have given my poems, sometimes in different versions, a bienvenida:

The Acentos Review: "Preparations for a Trip Home"

Adroit Journal: "Midwestern Skulls for the Broken Latino"

Breakwater Review: "After the Tempest," "Marrow (Then a wealthy Israeli student with a modeling career)," and "Marrow (The two-hearted spirit-spider generates blood)"

The Collapsar: "Queerodactyl (We vogued in graveyards, headstones big)" and "Queerodactyl (What we momentarily dubbed permission)"

Connotation Press: "Atonement in the Key of Padre"

Juked: "Queerodactyl (Bones classified as those of a seafarer)" and "Queerodactyl (With droopy but *WORK IT GIRL* wings, Queerodactrix)"

Meridian: "Quinceañera"

Platypus Press's *wildness*: "Queerodactyl (Mother is anti-devolution, present past)" and "Queerodactyl (Woke up like strangulated terracotta)"

Poetry: "Queerodactyl (Jewelry boom box spittin' *bidi bidi bom bom*)," "Queerodactyl (My heart was a dystopian)," "Queerodactyl (Spandex leggings authenticating my anaerobic)," and "Those Seventy-Two Bodies Belong to Us"

Public Pool: "Restored Mural for Orlando"

Reservoir: "When a Person Says Go Back to Your Country"

The Rumpus: "Catrachos" and "In Service of Silence"

Sibling Rivalry Press's *Assaracus*: "Amor Eterno," "Marero," "Marrow (They called you | Sarah | before you reared)," "Our Lady of Suyapa," and "Queerodactyl (You don't have to watch me whip my wings)"

Superstition Review: "PayDay Loan Phenomenology"

Up the Staircase Quarterly: "Arthur's Spelling Trubble"

Winter Tangerine: "Día de los Muertos"

Word Riot: "Finding Logic in a Crushed Head" and "Queerodactyl (After they locate and excavate your wing fossils)"

The Academy of American Poets republished "My Great-Grandmother's Egg Thief."

"Queerodactyl (We vogued in graveyards, headstones big)" was chosen by Natalie Diaz for *Best New Poets 2017*.

"Marero" and "Finding Logic in a Crushed Head" were republished in *Drunk Monkeys*.

"Restored Mural for Orlando" was republished in NPR's *Latino USA*, and mentioned in Melissa B. Warnke's "We can learn from the Orlando attack, but only if we're willing to be brave" in the *Los Angeles Times* and Jesse Lichtenstein's "How Poetry Came to Matter Again" in the *Atlantic*. It was also turned into a chapbook (Queerodactyl Press) to raise funds for the victims of the 2016 Pulse nightclub shooting in Orlando.

"Midwestern Skulls for the Broken Latino" and "Amor Eterno" appear in *The Wandering Song: Central American Writing in the United States* (Tia Chucha Press).

"Self-Portrait According to George W. Bush" appears in *IMANIMAN: Poets Writing in the Anzaldúan Borderlands* (Aunt Lute Books). An excerpt appears on the NEA website.

***

None of these palabras would exist without the extensive support, friendship, courage, and faith others have given me.

Ántes que todo le quiero dar las gracias a mis ancestros que con ellxs no hubiera escrito sobre estas experiencias difíciles e importantes. Gracias a mi abuelo que me enseñó a leer y a tenerle tanto respeto a la literatura y a las artes. Gracias a mi bisabuela Rita por enseñarme a soñar.

Gracias Mamá por siempre apoyarme en todas las buenas y en las malas. Este libro contiene tanto dolor como también esperanza. Aunque revela muchísimos secretos nunca se olvida de demostrar todo lo bueno que me ha enseñado.

Gracias Don Alfredo por haber sido un padre que nunca se olvidó que tuviera algo que comer. Por usted he podido llegar donde estoy.

Gracias a mi familia en Honduras por mis primeras memorias y por nunca olvidarse de mí. Con ustedes comparto sus tragedias y sus triunfos.

Gracias a Ivi, Berni, and Liz for keeping me alive with meals, coffee, laughter, and perritas. I have died multiple times and been brought back by you.

Gracias a D. Allen because you have taught me things about the world and especially about myself that I otherwise wouldn't have learned without your kindness, compassion, and enthrallment. You are the emotional and spiritual coauthor of this book.

Gracias for your friendship and mentorship over the years, which made this book possible: Chris Del Vesco, Pilar Lopez, Sun Yung Shin, Dr. Gabriela Spears-Rico, Elliott H. Powell,

Aron Cobbs, Dr. Tamilia D. Reed, Natalie Laczek, Audrey Gradzewic, Su Hwang, Anaïs Deal-Márquez, Bernard Ferguson, Maitreyi Ray, Patrick Nathan, Michael Kleber-Diggs, Jackie Hilgert, Beth Mikel Ellsworth, Merle Geode, Brett Elizabeth Jenkins, Christina Collins, Lisa Marie Brimmer, Rebecca Lindenberg, Timothy Otte, Fiona Avocado, María Isabel Álvarez, Ernesto L. Abeytia, Jasminne Méndez, Lupe Méndez, Michael Torres, Marci Calabretta Cancio-Bello, Chris Martin, Mary Austin Speaker, Gretchen Marquette, Maya Chinchilla, Cathleen Chambless, Alexandra Algaze, Elizabeth Tannen, and Gabriel Arrazola.

Gracias for supporting my words in multiple forms: Michael Walsh, Miguel M. Morales, Marco Antonio Huerta, Anthony Frame, Carey Salerno, Alexandra Lytton Regalado, Sagirah Shahid, Patrick Werle, Marion Gomez, Julie Brooks Barbour, Joel Salcido, Francine Conley, Aaron King, Kathryn Kysar, Heid E. Erdrich, John E. Orduña, Yaddyra Peralta, Kelsey Castañeda, Diane Seuss, Julian David Randall, Susana Aguilar-Marcelo, Zack Lavoie, Davon Loeb, Georgia Bellas and Mr. Bear, Mariama J. Lockington, Beth Mayer, Amy Fladeboe, David Bayliss, Rodrigo Sanchez-Chavarria, Daniel Tran, Ariel Francisco, Joel Hernandez, Tariq Luthun, Caseyrenée Lopez, Simone Muench, Roger Fierro, Sarah Blake, Emma Trelles, Heidi Czerwiec, Chavonn Williams Shen, Anthony Ceballos, M. Wright, A. Saavedra, Lisa Mecham, Michael Rowe, Kenzie Allen, Peter LaBerge, Michael Hettich, Zack Finch, Lara Mimosa Montes, Dua Saleh, Marcelo Hernandez Castillo, Caitlin Neely, Jenn Givhan, Vanessa Angélica Villarreal, Eduardo C. Corral, Sarah Rafael García, Nneka Onwuzurike, Chris Gonzalez, Alex Lemon, Hieu Minh Nguyen, Chris Fischbach, Ruben Quesada, Sam Herschel Wein, Rica Highers, Kaveh Akbar, Jonterri Gadson, Whittier Strong, Rosebud Ben-Oni, Stephen J. Furlong, Donte Collins, Bob Sykora, Alex Vigue, John Manuel Arias, Danez Smith, Lise Quintana, Jennifer Maritza McCauley, Ashley M. Jones, Jasmin Rae Ziegler, Vincent Toro, Joe Jimenez, Omar Figueras, Amy Botula, Lena Moses-Schmitt, Katie Aliféris, Andrea Jenkins, Suzi F. Garcia, Alessandra Bava, Allie Marini, Rachel Moritz, Miguel Soto, Araceli Lopez Esparza, Connor Coyne, Gregg Shapiro, William Bartram, and Matt Mauch.

Michael Chuderski: Gracias for your boundless love via palabras, flowers, textos, and pure understanding. You ground me in ways that continue to fascinate me.

Vicki Nicolaev, Cyndy Allen Alarto, and Zach Doss: Gracias for all the wisdom you continue to share with me, even from other spectacular dimensions. You are always missed.

Gracias a la facultad de University of Minnesota's Department of English and the MFA Program in Creative Writing. I'd like to darle gracias, in a particular, a Julie Schumacher, Ray Gonzalez, Patricia Hampl, Sugi Ganeshananthan, Kim Todd, Eric Daigre, Charles

Baxter, and M. J. Fitzgerald. Gracias a Douglas Kearney and Kathryn Nuernberger. I owe a great deal to Holly Vanderhaar. Gracias to my fellow colleagues, especially D. Allen, Su Hwang, Jackie Hilgert, MJ Gette, Jonathon Atkinson, Jonathan Damery, Jordan K. Thomas, Miriam W. Karraker, Jenn H. Carter, Emily Strasser, Connor Stratton, Joe Harris, Jonathan Escoffery, Mike Alberti, Ben Meyerson, Kristin Collier, Alexis P. Zanghi, Liam Kane-Grade, Erica Berry, and John Costello.

Gracias a Jeff Shotts, Chantz Erolin, and everyone at Graywolf who believed in my book and decided to take a risk on it.

For your unwavering generosity, gracias Don Share and the Poetry Foundation, especially Ydalmi V. Noriega, Lindsay Garbutt, Holly Amos, and Fred Sasaki. Gracias Crescendo Literary. Gracias Bao Phi. Gracias Loft Literary Center. Mil gracias a Francisco Aragón and Letras Latinas. Gracias Arizona State University and the Virginia G. Piper Center for Creative Writing. Gracias Human Rights Program at the University of Minnesota. Gracias Gesell family. Gracias Minnesota State Arts Board. Gracias National Endowment for the Arts and the judges of the 2019 grants. Gracias to the folk at O, Miami and Reading Queer. Gracias Latinx Writers Caucus. Gracias to the editors at *Sundog Lit*. Gracias Pridelines.

Gracias to the 2017 Ruth Lilly and Dorothy Sargent Rosenberg Fellows for your light and love: Fatimah Asghar, Sumita Chakraborty, Cortney Lamar Charleston, and Emily Jungmin Yoon.

Gracias to my therapist and my psych nurse for reminding me to drink water and for helping me fly again.

Gracias to my exes because you did invest time and energy to keep me alive and I can never repay that.

Gracias to anyone who has touched my life and blessed it, even though you may not be a part of my communities anymore. Gracias to my Twitter and Facebook rollercoastin' fams.

Gracias to everyone who's fed me at Victor's, Butter, Caffetto, Wedge, Pizza Hut, Burger King, Popeyes, and Mon Petit Chéri. Gracias to the makers and server maintenance technicians of *The Division* and *Overwatch*.

And to every teacher, student, and reader of my work: You have taught me lecciones I continue to learn from. I hope I've made you proud!

ROY G. GUZMÁN received a 2019 fellowship from the National Endowment for the Arts and a 2017 Ruth Lilly and Dorothy Sargent Rosenberg Poetry Fellowship. Raised in Miami, Guzmán lives in Minneapolis, Minnesota.

The text of *Catrachos* is set in Scala Pro.
Book design by Rachel Holscher.
Composition by Bookmobile Design and Digital
Publisher Services, Minneapolis, Minnesota.
Manufactured by Versa Press on acid-free,
30 percent postconsumer wastepaper.